BRUSHSTROKES OF SEDUCTION

A provocative journey through art, passion,
and the delicate dance of power.

Fiona Harvey

Web-Fi

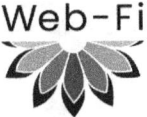

Copyright © 2024 Fiona De Brabanter

All rights reserved

The characters and events portrayed in this book are fictitious. Any similarity to real persons, living or dead, is coincidental and not intended by the author.

No part of this book may be reproduced, or stored in a retrieval system, or transmitted in any form or by any means, electronic, mechanical, photocopying, recording, or otherwise, without express written permission of the publisher.

Cover design by: Midjourney & Fiona De Brabanter

CONTENTS

Title Page
Copyright
Chapter 1 – The Narrator's Introduction   1
Chapter 2 – The Art of Seduction   15
Chapter 3 – The Road to Fontainebleau   31
Chapter 4 – Meeting Edward and Elodie   45
Chapter 5 – London Calling   60
Chapter 6 – Unexpected Revelations   72
Chapter 7 – The Art of Retreat   89
Epilogue   109
Afterword   111
Acknowledgement   113
About The Author   115

CHAPTER 1 – THE NARRATOR'S INTRODUCTION

The espresso's rich aroma mingled with the scent of fresh-baked croissants as Mordecai gazed out at the bustling Parisian street. His fingers absently traced the rim of his cup, mind drifting between the rhythmic flow of passersby and the glowing screen of his phone.

Dorothy's latest Instagram post flickered before him - a striking black and white portrait, her eyes piercing the camera with playful defiance. Mordecai's lips curled into a wry smile. How effortlessly she commanded attention, even through pixels and glass.

Always the provocateur, aren't you, ma chérie? he mused silently. *But I wonder if they see the vulnerability beneath that mask of boldness.*

His thumb hovered over the image, tracing the curve of her neck, the hint of collarbone peeking from her blouse. A familiar warmth spread through his chest, desire mingling with his customary detachment.

Mordecai set the phone down with a soft sigh. "Dangerous territory, old friend," he murmured to himself, taking another sip of espresso.

The café door chimed, and suddenly the air was alive with jasmine and possibility. Mordecai didn't need to look up to know it was her.

Dorothy swept in like a force of nature, all flowing silk and tousled curls. Her gauzy emerald blouse caught the sunlight, casting an otherworldly glow as she moved. One hand held her phone to her ear, the other gesticulating animatedly as she spoke.

"...yes, darling, exactly. A fusion of the digital and tactile. I want them to *feel* the pixels," she was saying, her voice a melody that turned heads throughout the café.

Mordecai watched, entranced despite himself, as Dorothy navigated the tables with effortless grace. The scent of her perfume - jasmine and something deeper, muskier - wafted past, leaving a trail of longing in its wake.

She caught his eye and winked, never breaking stride in her conversation. "We'll discuss more later. Ciao, bella."

Dorothy slipped her phone into her bag and approached Mordecai's table, a Mona Lisa smile playing on her lips. "Well, well," she purred. "If it isn't my favorite philosopher-king, holding court with the ghosts of Sartre and de Beauvoir."

Mordecai raised an eyebrow, fighting to maintain his air of nonchalance. "And here I thought I was communing with Camus.

Clearly, I need to work on my existential angst."

Dorothy laughed, the sound like wind chimes in a summer breeze. She slid into the chair across from him, crossing her legs with deliberate slowness. "Oh, I think you brood quite magnificently, *mon cher*. It's part of your charm."

"High praise indeed, coming from the queen of reinvention herself," Mordecai replied, gesturing to her outfit. "Another triumph of style over substance?"

Dorothy's eyes flashed, a mix of amusement and challenge. "You wound me, Mordecai. Don't you know that in our brave new world, the medium *is* the message?"

🌹

Mordecai leaned back, a wry smile playing on his lips. "Ah yes, McLuhan's ghost haunts us still. But tell me, Dorothy, when did you become so enamored with his theories? Last I checked, your preferred medium was more... tactile."

Dorothy's laugh was low and rich, sending a shiver down Mordecai's spine. "Always so quick to intellectualize, aren't you? Some things are meant to be felt, not dissected."

She reached across the table, her fingers brushing his as she stole a sip of his espresso. The casual intimacy of the gesture wasn't lost on Mordecai, and he felt a familiar tension coiling in his chest.

"Speaking of feeling," Dorothy continued, her voice dropping to a conspiratorial whisper, "I'm in the mood for some inspiration. Care to join me for a walk along the Seine?"

Mordecai hesitated, weighing the allure of Dorothy's company against his better judgment. Memories of their last "inspirational" outing flashed through his mind - the argument at the Louvre, the reconciliation on the Pont des Arts, the way her skin had glowed in the lamplight...

"Why not?" he found himself saying, surprising them both. "Someone needs to keep you tethered to reality."

As they left the café, Dorothy linked her arm through his, her warmth seeping through the fabric of his shirt. "Reality is overrated," she murmured. "I prefer the realm of possibility."

They strolled along the riverbank, the late afternoon sun casting long shadows across the water. Dorothy's perfume mingled with the scent of the river, creating an intoxicating blend that left Mordecai slightly dizzy.

"I've been thinking," Dorothy said suddenly, her eyes alight with excitement, "about staging a performance piece. Something that really pushes boundaries, you know?"

Mordecai's brow furrowed. "Boundaries of what, exactly? Taste? Legality?"

"Oh, don't be such a killjoy," she chided, nudging him playfully. "I'm talking about exploring the intersection of intimacy and technology. Imagine a live-streamed event where—"

"Where you blur the lines between public and private even further?" Mordecai interjected, his tone gentle but probing. "Dorothy, at what point does provocation become exploitation?"

She opened her mouth to retort, but her heel caught on an uneven cobblestone. Mordecai's arm shot out instinctively, catching her hand and steadying her. For a moment, they stood frozen, the contact electric between them.

🦢

Dorothy's fingers lingered in Mordecai's grasp as she regained her balance, her eyes meeting his with a mix of gratitude and challenge. "Exploitation? That's a loaded word, Mordecai. I prefer to think of it as... illumination."

She withdrew her hand slowly, but the warmth of her touch lingered on his skin as they resumed their walk. Mordecai fought to keep his voice steady. "Illuminate what, exactly?"

"The artifice of our digital personas," Dorothy explained, her voice taking on a passionate edge. "I'm envisioning an augmented reality installation. Visitors will enter a space where their online profiles are projected onto the walls, overlapping and interacting in real-time."

Mordecai's eyebrows rose. "Ambitious. And potentially invasive."

"That's the point," Dorothy countered. "As they move through the space, their digital selves will start to... glitch. Revealing the cracks in our carefully curated online identities."

They reached the Pont des Arts, and Dorothy paused, leaning against the railing. The setting sun painted the Seine in hues of gold and crimson, mirroring the fire in her eyes as she gazed out over the water.

Mordecai studied her profile, noting the slight furrow in her brow that belied her usual confidence. "It's provocative," he admitted. "But are you prepared for the backlash? People guard their online personas fiercely."

Dorothy's laugh held a hint of bitterness. "People guard illusions, Mordecai. I want to shatter them."

She turned to face him, her expression suddenly vulnerable. "Sometimes I feel like that river," she said softly, gesturing to the Seine. "Always moving, never still. Unable to find an anchor."

Mordecai felt a tug of empathy, mixed with a familiar sense of both attraction and trepidation. He chose his next words carefully. "Perhaps the beauty lies in the flow itself, Dorothy. Not every journey needs a destination."

Dorothy's eyes glimmered with mischief as she turned to Mordecai, a playful smirk tugging at her lips. "Oh, Mordecai," she purred, her voice a silky caress, "always the philosopher. Don't you ever get tired of living in that brilliant head of yours?"

Mordecai felt a familiar warmth bloom in his chest, equal parts exhilaration and wariness. "Someone has to be the voice of reason in this duo," he quipped, his tone dry but affectionate.

"Reason?" Dorothy scoffed, stepping closer. Her perfume, a heady blend of jasmine and something uniquely her, enveloped him. "I dare you to be unreasonable, just once. Let's see what that looks like on you."

Her fingers ghosted along his arm, leaving a trail of goosebumps in their wake. Mordecai's breath caught, his mind racing with the possibilities her challenge presented.

"What did you have in mind?" he asked, cursing the slight tremor in his voice.

Dorothy's eyes sparkled. "Pose for me. Right here, right now. I want to capture this moment, this... tension." She pulled out her phone, already opening a sketching app.

Mordecai hesitated, acutely aware of the tourists milling about. "Here? Now?"

"Yes, darling. Be my muse. Be spontaneous."

With a resigned sigh that didn't quite mask his intrigue, Mordecai struck an exaggerated pose against the bridge's railing. Dorothy's delighted laugh was worth the stares from passersby.

As Dorothy's fingers danced across her screen, Mordecai marveled at how easily she drew him out of his comfort zone. It was thrilling and terrifying in equal measure.

Dorothy lowered her phone and glanced at Mordecai with a conspiratorial smile. "You're quite the natural," she teased, tucking the device into her bag. "But come, there's so much more Parisian magic to uncover tonight."

Mordecai raised an eyebrow, a mixture of curiosity and caution flickering across his features. "Magic, you say?"

She leaned in, her voice a sultry whisper. "There's a rooftop gallery not far from here. Exclusive, electric, and... deliciously avant-garde. I think you'll find it enlightening."

Before he could protest, Dorothy looped her arm through his and began leading him down the cobblestone street. The hum of the Seine faded behind them as they wove through Paris's labyrinthine alleys, their laughter mingling with the evening breeze. The streets narrowed, lanterns casting golden pools of light that seemed to follow them like eager spectators.

By the time they reached the gallery's discreet entrance, Mordecai felt a strange combination of exhilaration and unease. The bouncer, a towering man with an impeccably tailored suit, nodded at Dorothy without question. She winked at him as they stepped inside, and Mordecai realized with a start that she was as much a part of this world as it was a part of her.

The scene shifted abruptly as they entered the rooftop gallery, the Parisian skyline a glittering backdrop to the avant-garde soirée. Mordecai blinked, momentarily overwhelmed by the sensory assault – pulsing music, the chatter of the city's artistic elite, and a dizzying array of multimedia installations.

Dorothy, however, was in her element. She glided through the crowd, her presence electric. Mordecai watched as heads turned, conversations paused, all eyes drawn to her magnetic allure.

"Isn't it marvelous?" she called back to him, gesturing to a nearby VR installation where guests donned headsets, their movements creating swirls of color on a massive screen.

Mordecai nodded, trailing in her wake. He observed the way she effortlessly engaged with everyone – a touch here, a whispered word there. It was a masterclass in social dynamics, and he couldn't help but admire her skill.

"Dorothy, darling!" A flamboyant artist embraced her. "You must tell me about your next project!"

As Dorothy launched into an animated description, Mordecai felt a familiar pang. He was her confidant, her intellectual sparring partner, but in moments like these, he was reminded of the vast, glittering world she inhabited – a world where he often felt like an outsider looking in.

Yet as the night wore on, he noticed how her gaze would seek him out across the room, how she'd return to his side, sharing private jokes and observations. It was a delicate dance, and Mordecai found himself, as always, irresistibly drawn into her orbit.

Mordecai found himself drifting towards a quieter corner of the rooftop, where a fellow guest – a lanky man with thick-rimmed glasses – was examining a holographic art piece with intense focus.

"Fascinating, isn't it?" Mordecai remarked, gesturing towards the shimmering display. "The way it blurs the line between the tangible and the virtual."

The man turned, his eyes lighting up at the prospect of intellectual discourse. "Absolutely. It's a perfect metaphor for modern relationships, don't you think?"

Mordecai raised an eyebrow, intrigued. "How so?"

"Well," the man began, "in this digital age, our connections are often as ephemeral as these holograms. We swipe, we match, we form instant intimacies that can vanish at the touch of a button."

Mordecai nodded, his mind drifting to Dorothy. "True. But doesn't that commodification of intimacy rob us of something essential?"

"Perhaps," the man mused. "Or maybe it's simply evolving. After all, desire has always been a complex dance of proximity and distance."

As they delved deeper into the discussion, Mordecai felt a familiar intellectual thrill. Yet part of him remained acutely aware of Dorothy's presence across the room, her laughter carrying over the ambient music.

Later, as the party began to wind down, Mordecai found himself alone with Dorothy on a secluded balcony. The city of Paris sprawled before them, a glittering tapestry of lights and shadows.

Dorothy leaned against the railing, her profile etched in moonlight. "Sometimes I wonder if any of it's real," she said softly.

Mordecai turned to her, surprised by the vulnerability in her voice. "What do you mean?"

She sighed, running a hand through her hair. "All of this. The parties, the adoration, the constant performance. I feel like I'm trapped in a persona of my own making."

Mordecai's heart constricted at the raw honesty in her words. He longed to reach out, to offer comfort, but held back. "You've always seemed so at ease with it all," he said carefully.

Dorothy's laugh was tinged with bitterness. "That's the trick, isn't it? But lately, I find myself craving something real. Something that isn't filtered through screens or expectations."

Mordecai swallowed hard, acutely aware of the electricity crackling between them. "Real can be terrifying," he murmured, his voice low.

Dorothy turned to him, her eyes searching his face. "Is that why you keep your distance, Mordecai? Fear of what's real?"

The question hung in the air, charged with unspoken longings. Mordecai's pulse quickened as he struggled to find the right words, knowing that his response could irrevocably alter the delicate balance of their relationship.

🐦

Mordecai's gaze lingered on Dorothy's face, tracing the contours illuminated by the soft Parisian night. He inhaled deeply, the scent of her jasmine perfume mingling with the crisp air.

"Perhaps," he admitted, his voice barely above a whisper. "But I also admire your boldness, Dorothy. The way you throw yourself into life with such abandon... it's intoxicating."

Dorothy's lips curled into a bittersweet smile. "And I envy your groundedness. The way you observe, analyze, find meaning in the chaos. Sometimes I feel like I'm just... drifting."

Mordecai stepped closer, drawn by an invisible thread. "We all drift sometimes. But you, Dorothy, you create ripples wherever you go.

You inspire change."

She laughed softly, the sound tinged with vulnerability. "Change, yes. But at what cost?"

Their eyes met, and Mordecai felt a surge of warmth in his chest. "Maybe that's where we balance each other," he mused.

Dorothy's eyes suddenly lit up with that familiar spark of mischief. "Speaking of balance... Mordecai, let's shake things up. How about a road trip?"

He blinked, caught off guard. "A road trip? Now?"

"Why not?" she challenged, her voice brimming with excitement. "We could just get in the car and drive. No plan, no destination. Just... freedom."

Mordecai hesitated, his mind racing through all the logical reasons to decline. Work commitments, responsibilities, the sheer impracticality of it all. But as he looked at Dorothy, her eyes alight with possibility, he felt the familiar pull of her magnetic presence.

"Come on," she coaxed, a teasing lilt in her voice. "Live a little, Mordecai. Step out of that comfort zone of yours."

He chuckled, shaking his head in amused disbelief. "You're incorrigible, you know that?"

Dorothy grinned, sensing victory. "Is that a yes?"

Mordecai paused, acutely aware of the crossroads before him. The sensible path beckoned, safe and predictable. But the allure of adventure, of uncharted emotional territory with Dorothy, was irresistible.

With a wry smile, he nodded. "Yes. God help me, but yes."

༃

As we stepped out of the soirée into the cool Parisian night, the city's twinkling lights seemed to mirror the sparkle in Dorothy's eyes. I couldn't help but marvel at the enigma walking beside me, her presence both electrifying and unsettling.

"So, where to first on this grand adventure of ours?" I asked, my tone a mixture of curiosity and trepidation.

Dorothy's laugh rang out, clear and melodious. "Oh Mordecai, always needing a plan. The whole point is not knowing, remember?"

I watched her as she twirled playfully on the sidewalk, her silhouette graceful against the cityscape. My mind raced with conflicting thoughts.

"You do realize," I said, "that spontaneity isn't exactly my strong suit."

She paused, turning to face me with a mischievous grin. "And that, my dear, is precisely why you need this."

I sighed, running a hand through my hair. "Dorothy, you're like a force of nature. Beautiful, unpredictable, and potentially destructive."

"Is that your roundabout way of saying I'm irresistible?" she teased, stepping closer.

The scent of her perfume enveloped me, jasmine with a hint of something darker. I felt my resolve wavering.

"It's my way of saying you're dangerous," I murmured, acutely aware of our proximity.

Dorothy's eyes softened for a moment, a flicker of vulnerability beneath her usual bravado. "Maybe we're dangerous for each other, Mordecai. But isn't that part of the thrill?"

I couldn't argue with that. As we continued walking, the weight of the decision we'd just made settled over me. This journey with Dorothy promised excitement, passion, and quite possibly, heartbreak. Yet I found myself drawn inexorably forward, like a moth to a flame.

"You know," I mused aloud, "there's a fine line between adventure and recklessness."

Dorothy linked her arm through mine, her touch sending a familiar shiver down my spine. "And we, my dear Mordecai, are about to dance all over that line."

As we disappeared into the Parisian night, I couldn't shake the feeling that I was stepping into something far bigger than a simple road trip. Dorothy's allure had always been my greatest weakness and my most exhilarating challenge. Now, it seemed, it would be my guide into uncharted territory – both geographical and emotional.

CHAPTER 2 – THE ART OF SEDUCTION

The soft glow of candlelight danced across Dorothy's face as she leaned forward, her eyes gleaming with mischief. The Parisian café hummed with hushed conversations and the rich aroma of espresso. Dorothy's slim fingers brushed the rim of her coffee cup, the light catching on her delicate gold bracelet.

"Oh Mordecai, you won't believe the night I had last week," she purred, her voice low and enticing. She pulled out her phone, manicured nail tapping the screen. "Here, let me show you..."

Dorothy tilted the phone towards me, revealing a dimly lit video. Pulsing lights flashed across writhing bodies on a crowded dance floor. My eyebrows raised as I caught a glimpse of Dorothy's lithe form in a shimmering dress, disappearing behind a velvet curtain with a tall, dark stranger.

"My my, you have been busy," I remarked dryly, unable to tear my eyes away.

Dorothy's laughter sparkled like champagne. "You have no idea. This club, Mordecai - it was unlike anything I've experienced before."

She set down her phone, leaning in conspiratorially. I found myself mirroring her posture, drawn into her orbit.

"Picture this," she began, her voice taking on a dreamy quality. "Strobe lights bouncing off mirrored walls, creating infinite reflections. The air thick with fog and desire. And the music - oh, the music! A pounding bass that vibrates through your entire body."

I could almost feel the beat myself, carried away by Dorothy's vivid description.

"I was wearing that silver sequined dress - you know the one. It caught every flash of light as I danced." Her fingers trailed along her collarbone, lost in the memory. "That's when I saw him watching me from across the room."

"The man from the video?" I asked, my curiosity piqued.

Dorothy's smile was enigmatic. "Perhaps. Let's just say he was tall, dark, and entirely too tempting to resist."

I felt a familiar tug of both fascination and unease. Dorothy's exploits never failed to captivate, even as they left me questioning the wisdom of such reckless abandon.

"He beckoned me over to a hidden alcove," she continued. "The music faded as he pulled back a heavy curtain, revealing a secret room bathed in red light."

Dorothy's eyes met mine, glittering with remembered excitement.

"Oh Mordecai, the tension was electric. When our hands first touched, it was like a jolt of lightning."

I shifted in my seat, both drawn in and conflicted by her tale. Part of me envied Dorothy's boldness, while another part recoiled at the risks she took.

"And then?" I prompted, unable to resist hearing more.

Dorothy's smile turned coy. "A lady never kisses and tells. But let's just say it was a night I won't soon forget."

As she sipped her coffee, I found myself wondering - not for the first time - about the emotional toll of Dorothy's adventures. Did the thrill truly satisfy, or was it merely a temporary distraction from deeper longings?

But I kept these thoughts to myself, content for now to bask in the glow of Dorothy's infectious energy and let her stories transport us both to a world of sensual possibility.

As Dorothy's tale drew to a close, I leaned back in my chair, my piercing gaze fixed on her. The dim café light cast intriguing shadows across her face, accentuating the mischievous glint in her eyes. I couldn't help but smirk, a mixture of admiration and skepticism playing across my features.

"Did you ever pause to wonder," I began, my voice low and tinged with dry humor, "if you were seducing them, or if they were seducing you?"

Dorothy's eyebrow arched, a challenge accepted. She leaned forward, her fingers tracing the rim of her coffee cup. "Oh Mordecai, always the philosopher. Does it matter? The dance is what counts."

I chuckled, shaking my head. "The dance, as you call it, seems more like a high-stakes game of chess. One wrong move..."

"And that's precisely what makes it thrilling," she countered, her voice dropping to a sultry whisper. "Speaking of thrilling, let me tell you about my latest... encounter."

Her tone shifted, taking on a calculated edge that piqued my interest. I leaned in, despite myself.

"There's this tech mogul, Ethan," Dorothy began, her eyes gleaming. "He's made billions with his AI startups, but now he's funding avant-garde art projects. We met at one of his gallery openings in New York."

I couldn't help but picture the scene – Dorothy, resplendent in some daring gown, captivating the room. "And how did you manage to stand out in a sea of aspiring artists and sycophants?"

She laughed, a melodic sound that turned heads at nearby tables, her allure impossible to ignore. "By being utterly disinterested in his money, of course," she said, swirling the wine in her glass. "Nothing intrigues a man like that more than someone who doesn't seem to want anything from him."

Dorothy leaned back, her posture effortless yet commanding, her fingers trailing lazily along the stem of her glass. As she continued, her words carried the weight of someone who knew exactly how to command attention.

"He invited me to his penthouse," she murmured, her voice dipping into a lower register that drew me closer. "You should have seen it, Mordecai—floor-to-ceiling windows, the entire city spread out below like a sea of liquid gold. I stepped inside, and for a moment, I just stood there, letting it wash over me. The height, the view, the sheer decadence of it all." She paused, her lips curving into a teasing smile. "And he stood behind me, watching."

I shifted in my seat, my curiosity and unease warring with each other. Dorothy always played her games well, but this felt different—more intense, somehow. "And then?" I prompted, my voice sounding far steadier than I felt.

Her smile widened, a glimmer of mischief and something darker flickering in her eyes. "I turned to him," she said, her tone almost conspiratorial. "And as I leaned in, I whispered, 'I know what you really want.'"

I leaned forward instinctively, caught in the web of her narrative. "And what did he do?"

Dorothy's fingers brushed her collarbone, her gaze distant, as though she were savoring the memory. "He froze," she said softly. "Just for a heartbeat. Then he stepped closer, his breath catching, his pupils blown wide. The power in that moment, Mordecai... it was intoxicating."

Her voice grew more intimate, the world around us fading. "I let him kiss me first," she confessed, her lips curving in satisfaction. "His hands were tentative, reverent, as though I might shatter under his touch. But that wasn't what he wanted. He needed someone to strip away the armor he wore for the world, to demand more."

I swallowed, the air between us charged. "And did you?"

"Oh, darling," she drawled, her eyes locking with mine, "I took everything."

Expanded Penthouse Encounter

"I turned to him fully, letting the silk of my dress slip down one shoulder, a deliberate invitation," Dorothy continued, her voice a sultry whisper. "His breath hitched, and that hesitation, that split-second vulnerability—it was like fuel to a fire."

She leaned forward slightly, her hands curling around her glass as though to steady herself against the memory. "I slid my arms around his neck, drawing him in until there was no space between us. His lips met mine, hesitant at first, then insistent. I pushed him back against the cool glass of the window, the city's lights framing us like an audience. His hands roamed, clumsy but eager, as though he didn't know where to start."

I remained silent, caught in the vivid intimacy of her recollection.

"'Is this what you wanted?' I whispered, trailing my nails down his chest, feeling his heartbeat thunder beneath my touch. He nodded, barely able to form words. And so, I made him earn it."

Her voice dipped lower, her words painted in slow, deliberate strokes. "I undid his tie with agonizing precision, then his shirt. Each button felt like a challenge, a reminder that I was in control. When he stood there, bare to me, I let my dress fall to the floor, and the way his eyes devoured me—it was exquisite."

Dorothy's smile turned wicked, her tone gaining an edge of playful cruelty. "I guided him to his knees, Mordecai. Right there, on the plush rug, with the city stretched out below us. He looked up at me as though I were the answer to every question he'd ever dared to ask."

I cleared my throat, the tension in her story pressing heavily against my chest. "And you?"

Her expression softened, a hint of vulnerability breaking through her carefully constructed veneer. "I made sure he understood that surrender isn't weakness—it's the purest form of trust."

Her next words were barely above a whisper, but they hit like a confession. "His mouth... his hands... he worshiped me, Mordecai. I let him explore every inch of me, guiding him when he faltered, teasing when he hesitated. I wanted him to feel the edges of his desire, to taste the freedom of letting go."

"And when he finally stood again," she said, her voice trembling just enough for me to notice, "I let him take control—briefly. We moved together, against the glass, against the city's glittering gaze. It was raw and messy and utterly consuming."

Dorothy leaned back, the spell of her tale unraveling but leaving a lingering heat in its wake. "And when it was over, he looked at me like I'd peeled back his skin and laid his soul bare."

I stared at her, my thoughts a chaotic tangle of admiration, concern, and something else I couldn't quite name. "And what did you feel?" I asked, my voice quieter than intended.

Her smile turned wistful, her eyes meeting mine. "Power, connection... and maybe just a touch of sadness," she admitted. "Because no matter how intense the moment, it always fades."

The weight of her words hung between us, the air thick with unspoken truths.

I raised an eyebrow, my gaze fixed on Dorothy's face as she finished her tale. The dim cafe light caught the glint in her eyes, a mixture of triumph and something else—something less definable.

"Impressive," I said, my tone dry. "But I have to wonder, Dorothy, is the allure really about the connection? Or is it more about the sense of control?"

I leaned in closer, the rich scent of espresso mingling with her subtle perfume. My voice dropped, carrying an edge of challenge. "These adventures of yours—are they truly fulfilling, or just an exquisite distraction?"

Dorothy's laughter rang out, a sound both melodic and slightly brittle. "Oh, Mordecai," she said, reaching for her wine glass. "Always the philosopher. If life is fleeting, why shouldn't pleasure be, too?"

But as she spoke, I noticed her fingers toying with her earring, a tell I'd come to recognize. Her eyes, usually so direct, flickered away from mine for a moment.

"Besides," she continued, her voice softer now, "intense experiences are the spice of life. They make us feel alive."

I watched as she took a sip of wine, leaving a crimson stain on the glass. In that moment, I caught a glimpse of something beneath her confident exterior—a flicker of vulnerability, perhaps even loneliness.

"And feeling alive," I mused, "is that what you're really chasing? Or is it a way to keep other feelings at bay?"

Dorothy's smile faltered for just a second before she recovered. "Always so perceptive, darling. It's what makes you dangerous."

❦

The dim light of the café cast long shadows across our table, mirroring the introspective turn our conversation had taken. I leaned back, fingers drumming lightly on the worn wood, and let out a soft chuckle.

"Dangerous? Perhaps. But not in the way you might think, Dorothy."

I paused, my eyes drifting to the rain-streaked window. The Parisian night beyond seemed to blur, much like the memories I was about to share.

"You know, there was a woman once," I began, my voice dropping to a near-whisper. "An artist I met in Barbizon. She had these eyes that seemed to capture the very essence of the forest—deep, mysterious, ever-changing."

Dorothy leaned in, her usual teasing demeanor softening into genuine curiosity. "Go on," she urged gently.

I sighed, a rueful smile playing at my lips. "We spent weeks circling each other. Every conversation was like a dance, each word carefully chosen. But I... I never made a move. I kept analyzing, overthinking, until one day she was simply gone."

My fingers tightened around my glass. "I often wonder what might have been if I'd allowed myself to be swept up in the moment, as you do."

Dorothy's eyebrows arched. "The great Mordecai, paralyzed by indecision? I can scarcely believe it."

I met her gaze, allowing a rare moment of vulnerability to show. "We all have our demons, don't we? Mine just happen to wear tweed and carry a pocket watch."

As I spoke, I noticed a change in Dorothy's demeanor. The sharp edges of her usual persona seemed to soften, her eyes reflecting a mix of empathy and something deeper—recognition, perhaps.

Dorothy's lips curled into a mischievous smile, her eyes glinting with renewed vigor. "Well, my dear Mordecai, allow me to paint you a picture that's far from indecision." She leaned back, crossing her legs with a fluid grace that drew my gaze.

"Venice," she began, her voice taking on a hushed, conspiratorial tone. "Carnival. The air thick with mystery and possibility."

I found myself leaning in, captivated despite my usual reservations.

"Picture this," Dorothy continued, her words weaving an intricate tapestry. "Midnight. The canals shrouded in mist. I'm wearing a gown of midnight blue, my face hidden behind an ornate mask of silver and peacock feathers."

Her fingers traced the rim of her wine glass, the gesture hypnotic. "I slip away from the crowds," Dorothy began, her voice low and intoxicating, "following a stranger in a golden mask.

His movements are deliberate, purposeful, as though he's been waiting for this moment all evening."

I could almost see it—the shimmer of her gown catching the faint moonlight, her heels clicking against the cobblestones, the air alive with the promise of secrecy. "We find a hidden alcove, shielded from the revelry outside. The stones are cool against my back as he presses me gently against them, his hands bracketing my waist, his breath warm against my neck."

Dorothy's gaze turned inward, her voice dropping to a husky murmur. "I barely had time to catch my breath before his lips found mine—hungry, insistent, yet careful not to cross boundaries I hadn't yet set. The golden mask shifted slightly, and for a fleeting moment, I considered removing it. But the anonymity of it all... it was electrifying."

She paused, a sly smile curving her lips. "His hands found the ties at the back of my gown, unfastening them with a skill that suggested he'd done this before. The fabric slipped down my shoulders, pooling silently at my feet. He took his time, his gaze raking over me like an artist admiring his masterpiece, his fingertips grazing my skin in a way that made me shiver."

I swallowed hard, but she wasn't done.

"In that tiny alcove, we became nothing but bodies and desire. His lips trailed down my collarbone, his teeth grazing my skin just enough to send sparks through me. My hands found his mask, but instead of removing it, I tilted his head back, exposing his throat. I wanted to taste him, to feel his pulse beneath my tongue, to remind him that power in moments like these is never one-sided."

Dorothy's fingers drummed softly against the table, her eyes shimmering with the memory. "I slid my hands beneath his jacket, pushing it from his shoulders, and ran my nails down his chest through the thin fabric of his shirt. He gasped—low, guttural—

before spinning me around, my palms braced against the cold stone. The contrast between his heat and the chill of the wall sent a jolt straight through me."

She leaned back in her chair, her smile wicked now. "And there, in the shadows, we lost ourselves completely. The world outside the alcove faded into nothing. Every touch, every sound was amplified—the way his hands gripped my hips, the sharp inhale when I pressed back against him, the undeniable rhythm we found as though we'd been made for that precise moment."

Dorothy's breath hitched slightly, her control slipping just enough for me to notice. "When it was over, when the fire between us finally ebbed, we stayed there for a moment—silent, disheveled, and utterly anonymous. And then, with a single whispered word, he disappeared into the night, leaving me to gather my gown and return to the masquerade as though nothing had happened."

I cleared my throat, my own breath slightly uneven. "You paint quite the picture, Dorothy," I said, my tone careful. "But I can't help but wonder—in all these grand seductions, how often do you truly let yourself be seduced? Without orchestrating every move, without playing director?"

The question hung in the air, heavy with implication. Dorothy's gaze flicked to mine, her smile faltering just slightly—a crack in her carefully cultivated mask of confidence.

Dorothy's gaze drifted to the window, her fingers pausing on the stem of her wine glass. The rain outside streaked the pane, mirroring the contemplative furrow of her brow. She lifted the glass to her lips, taking a slow, deliberate sip. When she lowered it, a faint red stain lingered on her lower lip.

"Sometimes," she began, her voice uncharacteristically soft, "I wonder what it'd feel like to stop running."

The admission hung in the air, fragile and unexpected. I leaned in, drawn by this rare glimpse of vulnerability.

Dorothy's eyes met mine, a flicker of something raw and unguarded in their depths. "The thrill is intoxicating, Mordecai. But when the mask comes off, when the stranger fades into the night... there's an emptiness." Her finger traced a raindrop's path down the window. "A yearning for something... more substantial."

I felt a tightening in my chest, a mix of empathy and an emotion I couldn't quite name. "And what would that 'something more' look like?" I asked, my voice low.

She turned back to me, a wry smile playing at the corners of her mouth. "That's the terrifying part, isn't it? The unknown."

Dorothy leaned closer, her perfume – a heady mix of jasmine and something darker – enveloping me. "We both know desire is messy, Mordecai," she murmured, her voice soft but firm. "Why else do you stay tangled in my world?"

The question struck me like a physical blow. I struggled to maintain my composure, acutely aware of the heat rising in my cheeks. Why indeed? The intellectual fascination? The vicarious thrill? Or something deeper, more dangerous?

"Perhaps," I managed, my voice slightly hoarse, "I'm drawn to the complexity. The contradictions." I paused, searching for the right words. "You're a puzzle I can't quite solve, Dorothy."

She laughed, a low, throaty sound that sent a shiver down my spine. "And you, my dear Mordecai, are the mirror I can't look away from."

The café had emptied around us, the soft clink of dishes and murmur of conversations fading into a hushed quiet. In the dimness, Dorothy's eyes seemed to gleam with an otherworldly light. Her fingers absently toyed with the delicate gold chain at her throat, the pendant nestled just above the swell of her breasts. I found my gaze drawn to the hypnotic movement, mesmerized by the play of shadows across her skin.

Beneath the table, my foot brushed against hers, an accidental touch that neither of us acknowledged but neither withdrew from. The connection, however slight, felt electric.

"You know," I began, breaking the companionable silence that had settled between us, "for all your tales of conquest and seduction, I wonder if you've ever truly allowed yourself to be vulnerable."

Dorothy's eyebrow arched, a challenge and an invitation in one. "Oh? And you think you have the key to unlocking that particular door, do you?"

I leaned forward, my voice dropping to match the intimacy of the moment. "You might burn brighter than the rest of us, Dorothy, but don't forget: flames need something to hold onto." I paused, watching the flicker of emotions play across her face. "Otherwise, they risk burning out entirely."

She stilled, her hand frozen mid-gesture. For a moment, I saw a glimpse of the woman behind the carefully constructed facade – uncertain, yearning, perhaps even a little afraid.

"And what would you suggest I hold onto, Mordecai?" she asked, her voice barely above a whisper.

I reached across the table, my fingers ghosting over hers. "That, my dear, is entirely up to you. But perhaps it's time to consider that the most exhilarating adventure might be allowing someone to truly know you."

Dorothy's gaze locked with mine, a silent battle of wills and unspoken desires raging between us. In that moment, I felt the delicate balance of our relationship shift, teetering on the edge of something new and terrifyingly profound.

🐚

Dorothy's lips curved into an enigmatic smile, her eyes sparkling with a newfound curiosity. She leaned back in her chair, her fingers toying with the delicate chain of her necklace. The low light of the café caught the mischievous glint in her eye, a silent acknowledgment of the weight of our conversation.

"You always did know how to cut right to the heart of things, Mordecai," she mused, her voice a low, rich timbre that sent a shiver down my spine. "It's infuriating... and oddly refreshing."

I watched as she gathered her things, the graceful movements a stark contrast to the vulnerability I'd glimpsed moments before. As she rose to leave, she paused, her hand resting lightly on the back of her chair.

"Maybe next time," Dorothy said, her gaze holding mine with an intensity that made my breath catch, "you'll tell me one of your stories. I can't help but wonder what secrets the great observer is keeping."

The invitation in her voice was unmistakable, layered with a complexity that spoke volumes about our evolving dynamic. As I watched her walk away, her hips swaying with that familiar confidence, I couldn't help but reflect on the dance we'd been engaged in for so long.

What would it mean, I wondered, *to truly let her in? To show her the parts of myself I've kept hidden, even as I've unraveled her mysteries?*

The possibility both thrilled and terrified me, a testament to Dorothy's unique ability to challenge my carefully constructed walls. As the door closed behind her, the lingering scent of her perfume a reminder of her presence, I found myself eagerly anticipating our next encounter, curious to see where this new understanding would lead us.

CHAPTER 3 – THE ROAD TO FONTAINEBLEAU

The purr of the engine vibrated through Dorothy's body as she gripped the leather steering wheel, her convertible slicing through the Parisian outskirts like a silver bullet. Wind whipped her hair into a frenzy, carrying with it the last vestiges of the city's perfume—a heady mix of espresso, cigarettes, and possibility.

She inhaled deeply, savoring the taste of freedom on her tongue. Her silk scarf, a vibrant splash of crimson against the cloudless sky, danced behind her like a banner of rebellion.

"Au revoir, mes amours," Dorothy murmured, a smirk playing at the corners of her lips. "Your gilded cage can't hold me anymore."

The warm sun caressed her skin, its golden fingers tracing the curve of her neck, the slope of her shoulders. Dorothy adjusted her sunglasses, catching a glimpse of herself in the rearview mirror. The woman staring back was wild, untamed—exactly how she wanted to be.

As the city faded into the distance, Mordecai's voice floated through her mind, unbidden and unwelcome. "Running away again, ma chérie?"

Dorothy gripped the wheel tighter, her knuckles whitening. "Not running," she whispered to the empty passenger seat. "Flying."

But Mordecai's presence lingered, like smoke clinging to silk. His voice, rich and layered with meaning, continued its gentle assault on her senses.

"Dorothy always claimed the road was her lover—unpredictable, intoxicating, and impossible to hold onto. Perhaps that's why I could never compete."

There was a note of longing in his tone that made Dorothy's heart clench. She pushed the accelerator harder, as if she could outrun the complications she'd left behind in Paris.

"You never tried to compete, mon cher," she thought, a mixture of affection and frustration coloring her inner dialogue. "You were too busy analyzing every move, every glance, every breath."

The speedometer climbed higher, matching the quickening of Dorothy's pulse. She was aware of every sensation: the vibration of the car beneath her, the rush of wind against her skin, the heady scent of summer-baked earth filling her lungs.

"Is this what you wanted, Mordecai?" she asked aloud, her words instantly swept away by the wind. "To see me stripped bare, vulnerable to the whims of the open road?"

But even as she posed the question, Dorothy knew the answer. This journey wasn't about Mordecai, or Paris, or anyone else. It was about her—her desires, her fears, her insatiable hunger for more.

A sign for the autoroute flashed by, and Dorothy made a split-second decision, veering onto the ramp. The world opened up before her, an endless ribbon of asphalt stretching towards the horizon.

"Oh, the places we'll go," she purred, a thrill of anticipation running through her body.

As if in response, Mordecai's voice whispered once more: "I'll be waiting, ma belle. Waiting to see what wonders—or wounds—you bring back from your grand adventure."

Dorothy laughed, the sound bright and sharp against the rush of the wind. "Then wait, my dear Casanova," she thought. "Wait and wonder. For this time, the story is all mine."

With that, she pressed the accelerator to the floor, leaving Paris—and all its entanglements—in a cloud of dust and possibility.

Dorothy's fingers drummed against the leather-wrapped steering wheel, her mind racing faster than the sleek convertible carrying her south. The hum of the engine vibrated through her, a low, persistent thrum that matched the restless beating of her heart.

"Reinvention," she murmured, tasting the word on her lips. "God, how I need it."

The rush of wind caressed her skin, teasing loose strands of hair from her artfully messy updo. Dorothy closed her eyes for a brief, dangerous moment, savoring the sensation.

"This," she thought, "this is what I've been missing. Not the touch of a man, but the touch of freedom itself."

Her eyes snapped open, catching sight of her reflection in the rearview mirror. The woman staring back was familiar, yet somehow different – wilder, more alive.

"He'd want to dissect this moment," Dorothy mused, Mordecai's face flashing unbidden in her mind. "Analyze my every impulse, my every fleeting desire."

She shook her head, banishing the thought. "But out here, there's no one to judge. No one to impress. Just me and the open road."

The landscape began to shift, urban sprawl giving way to undulating hills dotted with modern wineries and boutique farms. Dorothy navigated a series of curves, each turn revealing a new vista more breathtaking than the last.

"Mon Dieu," Dorothy murmured as the sun-drenched vineyards stretched endlessly before her. The air carried the intoxicating blend of lavender, sun-warmed earth, and the faint tang of crushed grapes. Slowing her convertible along the winding road, she finally pulled over at a sleek, glass-walled tasting room perched elegantly on the hillside.

As she stepped out of the car, the gravel crunched beneath her designer flats. A young sommelier emerged almost immediately, his crisp white shirt rolled neatly at the cuffs, his polished demeanor offset by a flicker of admiration as his gaze swept over her. "Bienvenue, madame," he greeted, his voice smooth and inviting. "Would you care to sample something truly exceptional?"

Dorothy's lips curved into a smile, her eyes glinting with intrigue. "Why not? Life is about indulging in the unexpected, don't you think?"

The sommelier's cheeks flushed faintly as he gestured toward a quiet corner of the tasting room. A polished bar gleamed in the sunlight streaming through the glass walls, a row of delicate crystal glasses awaiting their turn. Dorothy trailed her fingers along the cool marble of the counter, the touch grounding and luxurious.

He reached behind the bar, producing a bottle of crimson liquid that shimmered like molten rubies in the light. "This," he said, his voice rich with reverence, "is one of our rarest vintages. Complex, bold, and not for the faint of heart."

Dorothy tilted her head, a playful smile forming. "Faint-hearted has never been an adjective used to describe me."

Pouring the wine, he slid the glass toward her, his fingers brushing hers in the exchange. The brief touch sent a spark down her spine—electric, deliberate, and loaded with unspoken promise. Dorothy swirled the wine slowly, watching as its rich color painted the interior of the glass. She raised it to her lips, savoring the bold, full-bodied flavor as it coated her palate.

"Impressive," she murmured, lowering the glass. Her tone carried a subtle challenge. "But I'm not so easily seduced."

The sommelier leaned forward slightly, his grin widening, his eyes locked on hers. "Good," he replied, his voice a low rumble. "Neither am I."

Dorothy laughed, the sound melodic and teasing. "Then I suppose we have something in common." Her fingers danced lightly over the rim of her glass as she met his gaze unflinchingly.

The room around them seemed to fade, the only anchors the wine's heady aroma and the magnetic pull between them. For a moment, Dorothy considered pushing the flirtation further—testing the boundaries of this charged encounter—but instead, she lifted her glass in a silent toast, her enigmatic smile speaking volumes.

"To bold flavors and bold choices," she said lightly, her words layered with meaning.

The sommelier inclined his head, his smile lingering as she turned back to the view of the vineyards below, the wine glass cradled delicately in her hand. As the sun dipped lower on the horizon, casting a golden glow across the vines, Dorothy felt the stirrings of something both exhilarating and entirely new.

"To adventure," she murmured, bringing the wine to her lips.

The liquid rolled over her tongue, bold and dark, leaving a whisper of heat. She smiled, wondering if she could bottle this moment as easily as the wine.

"Exquisite," Dorothy purred, locking eyes with the sommelier. "I do hope you have more where that came from."

As she savored the wine, her thoughts drifted to Mordecai. What would he make of this scene? Of her?

Mordecai's voice, rich with admiration and a hint of something darker, echoed in her mind:

"Dorothy always had a way of making herself at home, whether in a Parisian salon or a sun-drenched vineyard. She moved through life as if she belonged everywhere and nowhere. I envied her freedom, even as I resented how easily she could leave me behind."

Dorothy set down the glass, a familiar restlessness stirring within her. The sommelier's inviting smile promised a delightful distraction, but was it enough to quell her constant craving for something more?

"Another taste?" he asked, already reaching for the bottle, the rich crimson liquid catching the late afternoon light.

She hesitated, caught between desire and the allure of the unknown. Her eyes swept the room, noting the carefully curated displays of rare vintages and artisanal accompaniments—delicate cheeses, jars of golden honey, and dark chocolate truffles arranged like treasures.

"Perhaps," Dorothy replied, her voice a silken tease. "But tell me, what other secrets does this tasting room of yours hold?"

The sommelier's lips curved into a knowing smile, his gaze flicking toward a discreet doorway at the edge of the room. "If you're looking for secrets, madame, I might just have something... extraordinary for you."

Dorothy's curiosity piqued, her pulse quickening as she followed his gaze. "Lead the way," she said softly, her tone laced with anticipation.

🦢

Dorothy's heels clicked against the sun-warmed stones as she approached the boutique vineyard nestled among rolling hills. The air was heavy with the scent of ripening grapes and earthy tannins. A ruggedly handsome man with sun-kissed skin and piercing green eyes greeted her, his smile warm and inviting.

"Bienvenue, mademoiselle," he said, his voice a rich baritone. "I'm Claude, the vintner. What brings such a sophisticated beauty to our humble vineyard?"

Dorothy's lips curved into a coy smile. "The promise of exquisite wine and... stimulating company," she purred, her eyes meeting his with unmistakable heat.

Claude chuckled, leading her to a secluded tasting area tucked behind a curtain of ivy. The air was cooler here, tinged with the faint, earthy aroma of aging barrels. "Then allow me to introduce you to our most seductive vintage," he said, pouring a deep crimson wine into a crystal glass.

As he leaned close to set the glass before her, Dorothy could feel the warmth of his breath on her neck. "This wine," he murmured, his voice low, "is said to awaken the deepest desires."

Dorothy took a slow sip, letting the complex flavors dance on her tongue before swallowing. "Mmm," she hummed, her voice thick with pleasure. "And what desires might those be, I wonder?"

Claude's fingers brushed a stray lock of hair from her face, lingering a moment too long. His gaze locked on hers, filled with unspoken promise. "Perhaps," he suggested, "we could explore that together."

Dorothy leaned in, her lips nearly grazing his ear. "Oh, Claude," she whispered, her voice a velvet caress, "your wine may be an aphrodisiac, but I assure you, I need no such help in that department."

She leaned back, her eyes glittering with mischief, relishing the flush creeping up his neck. But before he could respond, Dorothy stood, trailing her fingers down his arm as she walked toward the barrel-lined wall. She stopped, glancing over her shoulder with a sultry smile.

"Are you going to stand there all day," she teased, "or are you going to show me just how... passionate a vintner can be?"

Claude followed her, his movements deliberate, as if savoring every step toward her. When he reached her, his hands gripped her waist, pulling her close. Their lips met in a fervent kiss, the taste of wine mingling with the electric heat between them. Dorothy's hands slid to his belt, her fingers deft as she unbuckled it.

She sank to her knees with practiced grace, her gaze locked on his as her hands worked his waistband loose. Claude exhaled sharply, his fingers threading into her hair as her lips found him, her movements unhurried but relentless. Each flick of her tongue, each calculated stroke, drew shuddering breaths from him, his control unraveling with every moment.

When Claude lifted her to her feet, his lips devoured hers with renewed urgency. He spun her against the barrel, hiking her silk skirt to her thighs. The first thrust stole her breath, a gasp escaping her lips as he filled her completely. Each movement was rough but deliberate, their rhythm intensifying as the sound of their passion mingled with the faint hum of distant cicadas.

When it was over, they leaned against each other, their breath heavy and uneven. Claude pressed a lingering kiss to her shoulder before stepping back, his hand brushing her cheek. Dorothy, ever composed, adjusted her skirt and smiled at him—a smile full of satisfaction and yet, unmistakably, farewell.

The sun had begun its slow descent as Dorothy walked back to her car, the gravel crunching under her heels. She slid into the driver's seat, the leather warm from the day's heat. For a moment, she sat in stillness, her fingers trailing over the steering wheel as she let the experience settle into her.

A small smile played at her lips. There was something intoxicating about the freedom of moments like these, of giving herself to the thrill without apology or consequence. Yet, as she started the car, a flicker of longing touched her—a whisper of something she couldn't yet name.

The engine purred to life, and the road unfolded before her like an endless ribbon of possibility. The vineyards faded into the distance, giving way to golden fields and lavender-scented air. She drove with the top down, the wind teasing her hair, her chest rising and falling with the rhythm of her breaths. The open road promised more stops, more encounters, more... everything.

When she reached the overlook, she pulled the car to a halt. Gravel crunched beneath the tires as she stepped out, her silk blouse billowing in the warm breeze. Dorothy walked to the edge, her fingers trailing along the rough stone barrier. The vista before her—rolling hills meeting the impossibly blue sky—was breathtaking.

She inhaled deeply, the lavender and sun-warmed earth filling her senses. The restlessness returned, a constant, familiar companion. As she gazed out, a thought whispered through her mind: What would it be like to stop fighting for control, to let someone—or something—take her completely?

The idea thrilled and terrified her. She closed her eyes, the sound of the wind and distant birdsong wrapping around her like a promise. For now, though, the road called, and Dorothy was always one to answer.

"Mordecai would have a field day psychoanalyzing this," she chuckled to herself, imagining his raised eyebrow and probing questions.

She closed her eyes, letting the warmth of the sun caress her face. "What do you think, Midi?" she asked the landscape. "Should I let go? Surrender to... whatever this is?"

The wind picked up, sending a shiver down her spine despite the heat. Dorothy opened her eyes, a small smile playing on her lips. "Maybe that's my answer," she mused.

As the sun began its descent, painting the sky in vibrant streaks of orange and pink, Dorothy reluctantly returned to her car. She slid behind the wheel, the leather seat warm against her skin.

"Time to chase that horizon," she murmured, starting the engine. As she pulled away from the overlook, the setting sun bathed everything in a golden glow, transforming the landscape into something almost ethereal.

Dorothy felt a surge of exhilaration as she navigated the winding road. "Look at you," she whispered to herself, "a goddess chasing the last rays of day." The thought made her laugh, but there was truth in it too. Here, in this moment, she felt powerful, beautiful, unstoppable.

The convertible hugged each curve of the road, and Dorothy reveled in the control, even as part of her longed to let go. It was a delicious contradiction, one that sent a thrill of anticipation through her for what lay ahead.

As twilight deepened, Dorothy's thoughts drifted, her grip on the steering wheel loosening. The purr of the engine and the rush of wind became a hypnotic lullaby, drawing her deeper into introspection.

"Freedom," she murmured, tasting the word on her lips. "Is that what I'm chasing?"

Her mind conjured Mordecai's voice, as clear as if he were sitting beside her. "And what exactly are you running from, Dorothy?"

She frowned, fingers tightening on the wheel. "I'm not running," she argued with the phantom. "I'm... exploring."

A sardonic chuckle echoed in her mind. "Semantics, my dear. You've always been good at those."

Dorothy sighed, her eyes fixed on the darkening road ahead. "Maybe I am running. But what's wrong with that? The world's too big, too full of possibilities to stay in one place."

"And yet," Mordecai's imagined voice persisted, "here you are, heading straight for Barbizon. Hardly seems like aimless wandering, does it?"

The truth of it stung. Dorothy bit her lip, considering. "I'm curious," she admitted to herself. "About Edward, about Elodie. About... what might happen."

As if on cue, the first twinkling lights of Barbizon appeared on the horizon. Dorothy felt a flutter in her stomach – excitement or apprehension, she couldn't quite tell.

The village emerged from the darkness like a mirage, quaint buildings and narrow streets bathed in the warm glow of streetlamps. Dorothy slowed the car, drinking in the sight.

"It's beautiful," she whispered, a smile tugging at her lips. The air had cooled considerably, carrying the scent of pine and something else – possibility, perhaps.

As she navigated the quiet streets, searching for her lodgings, a shiver ran through her that had nothing to do with the temperature. "Something's going to happen here," she murmured. "I can feel it."

The headlights of her car cut through the darkness, illuminating glimpses of the village – an old fountain, a charming café, the edge of the famous forest. Each sight seemed to whisper secrets, promises of adventure and discovery.

Dorothy pulled up to a small, elegant hotel. As she stepped out of the car, the chill in the air made her shiver despite herself. She looked up at the starry sky, feeling both small and significant.

"Well, Barbizon," she said softly, "I'm here. Show me what you've got."

༄

Mordecai leaned back in his well-worn leather chair, the faint creak of the aged upholstery filling the quiet of his study. The room was dimly lit, the glow of a single desk lamp pooling over an open notebook and a half-empty cup of coffee. Outside, Paris hummed faintly, the rhythm of the city a comforting backdrop.

In his hand, a sleek dictaphone glinted under the light. He held it to his lips, his tone measured but tinged with fondness and wry amusement. "Dorothy always had a knack for finding the extraordinary in the ordinary. It was one of her most infuriating and captivating traits."

Mordecai paused, swirling the coffee absently in its porcelain cup. He let the steam rise to his face as if coaxing his thoughts to form. "As I picture her now, standing beneath the star-studded sky of Barbizon, I can't help but feel a twinge of... something. Envy? Longing? Perhaps both."

His gaze drifted to the window, where the Eiffel Tower's beacon sliced through the darkness. "I've known Dorothy long enough to recognize that gleam in her eye, even from afar. It's the look of a woman on the precipice of something life-altering. The air in Barbizon is thick with artistic legacy and untold stories. For Dorothy, it might as well be catnip."

He set the coffee cup down, leaning forward to jot a quick note in his journal. The scratch of the pen punctuated his words as his tone grew more introspective. "Her journey isn't about fleeing Paris, or me, or even herself. No, Dorothy's odyssey is about discovery. She's like a moth drawn to the flame of experience, heedless of the potential for burns. And in the shadowed corners of Barbizon, I have a feeling she's about to uncover something truly extraordinary."

Mordecai chuckled softly, the sound warming the solitude of the room. "The question is, will she emerge from this adventure transformed... or consumed? Knowing Dorothy," he murmured, switching off the dictaphone, "it will be both."

He reclined in the chair, the notebook still open in front of him, a faint smile playing on his lips. Somewhere out there, Dorothy was chasing the extraordinary, and Mordecai, as always, found himself drawn into her orbit—even from miles away.

CHAPTER 4 – MEETING EDWARD AND ELODIE

The late afternoon sun cast a golden glow on the winding road ahead, where Edward's bohemian disarray and Elodie's serene poise stood out like a tableau vivant against the lush Midi landscape. Dorothy's lips curved into a knowing smile as she eased her foot off the accelerator. There was always something irresistible about the untold stories behind strangers' eyes.

She pulled over, rolling down the window. "Need a lift?" The playful lilt in her voice carried on the warm breeze.

Edward's face lit up, his paint-stained hands gesticulating wildly as he approached. "Mademoiselle, you are a vision! An angel of mercy on this dusty road."

Dorothy suppressed a chuckle at his dramatic flair. This one's an artist, no doubt. Her gaze flickered to the woman behind him, noting the quiet grace in her movements.

As Edward clambered into the backseat, the scent of turpentine and earthy oils filled the car. "You've rescued us from the purgatory of the mundane," he declared. "This view - it's art waiting to happen!"

"I'm glad to play muse to your inspiration," Dorothy replied, amusement coloring her tone. She watched in the rearview mirror as Edward leaned back, already lost in the passing landscape. His obliviousness was almost endearing.

"Where are you headed?" she asked, curiosity piqued by this mismatched pair.

Edward's response was typically poetic. "Wherever the light leads us, ma chérie. We chase the golden hour like butterflies pursuing the sun."

Dorothy bit back a smile. "How delightfully vague. Any particular direction in mind?"

As Edward launched into a meandering explanation involving ley lines and artistic pilgrimages, Dorothy's thoughts drifted. There was something intoxicating about chance encounters, the thrill of new connections sparking to life. It reminded her of her grandfather Émile's adventures, chronicled in those deliciously scandalous diaries she'd inherited.

She imagined what he'd say about this situation. 'Always follow your curiosity, ma petite. It will lead you to the most exquisite pleasures.'

The purr of the engine and Edward's lyrical musings faded into background noise as Dorothy's mind wandered to the possibilities that lay ahead. This impromptu road trip promised to be far more interesting than she'd anticipated.

Elodie slid into the passenger seat with a quiet elegance that immediately captivated Dorothy. The heady blend of sandalwood and rose that followed her filled the car, intoxicating in its subtlety. As Elodie's eyes met Dorothy's, cool yet inviting, Dorothy felt a familiar thrill of anticipation.

"Thank you for stopping," Elodie said, her voice low and melodious. "I'm Elodie."

Dorothy's pulse quickened at the careful pause before Elodie spoke, the slight tilt of her chin. "Dorothy," she replied, her own voice a touch huskier than usual. "It's my pleasure."

As they pulled back onto the winding road, Dorothy found herself hyper-aware of Elodie's presence beside her. The way her fingers lightly drummed on her thigh, the curve of her neck as she gazed out the window - each detail seemed magnified, electric.

Determined to keep Edward distracted, Dorothy steered the conversation toward his art. "Your work must be extraordinary, Edward. What inspires you most?"

Edward's eyes brightened, just as she'd intended. "Oh, the interplay of light and shadow, the raw emotion of a moment captured in time!" He launched into an impassioned monologue about his artistic process.

Dorothy nodded at appropriate intervals, but her focus had shifted entirely. From the corner of her eye, she caught Elodie's knowing smirk. A spark of understanding passed between them, unspoken but palpable.

I wonder what stories she holds, Dorothy mused, her imagination running wild with possibilities. *There's an ocean of depth behind those eyes, and I'm dying to dive in.*

As Edward's poetic ramblings filled the background, Dorothy allowed herself to be drawn into the quiet magnetism of Elodie's presence, savoring the delicious tension that hung in the air between them.

❦

The secluded manor emerged from the shadows, its ivy-clad walls illuminated by strategically placed garden lights. Dorothy guided the car up the winding gravel drive, her pulse quickening with each turn. "Mon dieu, it's like something out of a movie!" Edward exclaimed, practically bouncing in his seat.

Dorothy smirked, throwing a glance at Elodie. "Looks like someone's already found their muse for the evening."

The three of them stepped out of the car, their luggage thudding softly onto the driveway. Dorothy pulled a key from her pocket, its brass edges cool and heavy against her palm. "The caretaker said she left everything ready for us. This place hasn't had guests in a while, so don't expect five-star service."

Edward's eyes widened as they approached the massive oak doors, which creaked dramatically when Dorothy unlocked them. "Who cares about service when you have *this*? Look at the stonework!"

Inside, motion sensor lights flickered on, revealing soaring ceilings and a mix of antique and contemporary decor. A faint scent of polished wood and old books lingered in the air, grounding the manor in its history. Dorothy flipped through a welcome booklet left on a side table. "Wi-Fi password's here, by the way. Don't say I didn't think of everything."

"The Wi-Fi can wait," Edward called out, already exploring the foyer with his phone camera. "The light here! The textures! I need to document this before it fades."

Elodie trailed behind, glancing at the sleek, modern security panel by the door. "Are we sure this place isn't haunted? It's too perfect."

Dorothy rolled her eyes, her practical side taking over. "No ghosts. Just Airbnb magic and some very well-paid cleaners." She led them toward the staircase. "Come on. I'll show you to your rooms."

The wooden steps creaked under their feet, the sound echoing softly in the high-ceilinged hall. Dorothy's fingers trailed the banister, smooth from years of wear and care. "The listing mentioned this place used to host artists' retreats back in the 1930s. Think of all the creativity that's passed through here."

Edward didn't wait for further explanation, bounding ahead and throwing open a door. "I'm calling this room!" he announced, gesturing dramatically to the beams of light pouring through an arched window.

"Fine by me," Dorothy called back. "Just don't rearrange the furniture. I promised the owner we'd keep everything as is." She turned to Elodie. "There's another room down the hall. You take that one."

Elodie raised an eyebrow, her tone teasing. "And where's the mysterious Ms. Duval staying? The haunted attic?"

"Funny," Dorothy replied with a smirk. "I've got the master suite. Benefits of being the designated driver."

As Edward's excited exclamations filled the air, Dorothy lingered by the window, watching the last hues of twilight melt into night. She hadn't planned on hosting this impromptu getaway, but standing here, surrounded by the weight of history and inspiration, she felt an undeniable spark. Whatever the weekend held, it would be anything but ordinary.

Dorothy paused at the top of the stairs, watching as Edward disappeared into his assigned room, already fumbling for his sketchbook. She turned to find Elodie lingering behind her, a bemused smile playing on her lips.

"He's... enthusiastic," Elodie murmured, her voice low and rich.

"Quite," Dorothy agreed, suddenly aware of how close they were standing. "Though I find myself more intrigued by the quiet ones."

Elodie's eyebrow arched slightly. "Is that so?"

Dorothy leaned in, her voice dropping to a whisper. "They tend to have the most fascinating secrets."

The air between them crackled with possibility. Dorothy inhaled deeply, drinking in the moment, the atmosphere thick with the promise of untold pleasures.

"I should check on Edward," Elodie said softly, though she made no move to leave.

Dorothy nodded, stepping back with practiced nonchalance. "Of course. I'll be in the parlor, if either of you need anything."

As Elodie slipped away, Dorothy descended the stairs, her mind racing. This game of cat and mouse was intoxicating, but she knew better than to rush. The night was young, and anticipation was half the fun.

Dorothy settled into a plush armchair in the parlor, swirling a glass of deep red wine. The candlelight cast flickering shadows across the room, creating an intimate atmosphere that seemed to breathe with possibility. She couldn't help but smile, recalling the spark in Elodie's eyes moments ago.

Soft footsteps approached, and Elodie appeared in the doorway, a vision of quiet grace. "Edward's completely absorbed in his sketching," she said, her voice carrying a hint of fond exasperation. "I doubt we'll see him for hours."

Dorothy patted the seat beside her invitingly. "Then it seems we have some time to ourselves. Care to join me?"

Elodie hesitated for a heartbeat before gliding across the room, settling into the adjacent chair. Dorothy poured her a glass of wine, their fingers brushing as she handed it over.

"To unexpected encounters," Dorothy toasted, clinking their glasses gently.

Elodie's lips curved into a smile. "And to the stories they might tell."

As they sipped, Dorothy observed Elodie over the rim of her glass. The woman's fingers grazed the stem of her wineglass, movements deliberate and slow. Dorothy felt her own pulse quicken, mirroring the rhythm.

"Does he always get so lost in his art?" Dorothy asked, her voice low and tinged with curiosity.

Elodie's smile turned wistful. "It's one of the things I admire about him. And one of the things that drives me mad."

Dorothy leaned in slightly, intrigued. "Oh? Do tell."

Elodie's gaze dropped to her glass, swirling the wine thoughtfully. "Edward sees the world so vividly, with such passion. It's beautiful, really. But sometimes..." she trailed off, searching for words.

"Sometimes you wish that passion was directed elsewhere?" Dorothy supplied gently.

A faint blush rose to Elodie's cheeks. "Perhaps," she admitted softly.

Dorothy's mind raced, piecing together the unspoken nuances of Elodie's relationship with Edward. There was admiration there, certainly, but also a yearning for something more. Something Edward, in his artistic fervor, might be overlooking.

"And what about you?" Dorothy asked, her voice dropping to a near-whisper. "What drives you mad, Elodie?"

The question hung in the air, heavy with implication. Elodie's eyes met Dorothy's, a flicker of vulnerability passing through them.

"Perhaps... wanting things I shouldn't," Elodie murmured, the flush on her cheeks deepening.

Dorothy felt a thrill run through her at the admission. She leaned closer, her voice warm and inviting. "In my experience, those are often the most worthwhile things to want."

The air between them thickened, charged with an unspoken intensity that seemed to drown out the rest of the room. Dorothy leaned in slightly, her movements deliberate, her voice low enough to pull Elodie in. "Sometimes it's worth the risk," she murmured, the words slipping between them like a challenge.

Elodie's breath hitched, her pupils dilating as Dorothy's fingers brushed against the curve of her wrist. The contact was impossibly light, like the whisper of silk or the promise of something forbidden. It was such a small touch, and yet, it unraveled her. A visible shiver coursed through Elodie's body, her hand trembling as she set her wineglass down. The crystal chimed softly against the table, the sound unnervingly loud in the fragile quiet between them.

"I…" Elodie began, but the word fractured in her throat. Her gaze was locked on Dorothy, her lips slightly parted, as if the mere act of speaking was too great a task under the weight of that moment. The faintest sheen of vulnerability flickered in her eyes, a softness that Dorothy found intoxicating.

Dorothy's heart pounded in her chest, a relentless rhythm that matched the storm brewing in her thoughts. She was hyper-aware of Elodie's every move—the subtle rise and fall of her chest, the way her lashes cast shadows across her cheekbones. It was a kind of captivation she hadn't felt in years, an exquisite, dangerous thrill that pushed logic aside.

"What is it you truly want, Elodie?" Dorothy asked, her voice velvet and razor edges, slicing through the silence. Her thumb brushed against Elodie's pulse point, and she felt it there—a rapid flutter betraying what words couldn't. A slight smirk touched Dorothy's lips. She could taste the hesitation, the pull of fear and longing.

Elodie swallowed hard, her voice trembling. "I don't know," she whispered, though the truth of it burned in her expression. The admission hung between them, vulnerable and raw.

"Yes, you do," Dorothy countered, leaning closer. Her tone was almost a whisper now, dark and inviting. "You know exactly what you want. You're just afraid to take it."

Elodie's lips parted, but before she could speak, Edward's jubilant exclamation shattered the moment like glass dropped onto stone.

"Ah! The interplay of light and shadow!" His voice boomed from across the room, a burst of unfiltered enthusiasm that felt almost absurd in the charged intimacy of the moment.

Dorothy closed her eyes briefly, a flicker of irritation passing over her features. She chuckled softly, the sound tinged with disbelief. "Perfect timing, as always," she muttered, her gaze never leaving Elodie's face. The intensity between them hadn't dissipated, merely paused, like a coiled snake waiting to strike.

Elodie's lips curved into a faint smile, though the tension in her body hadn't eased. "You get used to it," she said, her voice softer now, carrying a note of shaky humor.

Edward's pencil scratched furiously against his sketchpad, the sound jarring in the otherwise quiet room. "The chiaroscuro effect here is simply magnificent!" he muttered, oblivious to the scene he'd interrupted.

Dorothy turned back to Elodie, her fingertips still resting on the other woman's wrist, this time pressing with slightly more intent. Her voice dropped lower, edged with something darker. "Perhaps we should continue this conversation somewhere less… theatrical," she suggested, her tone a deliberate invitation.

Elodie's smile faltered, her eyes searching Dorothy's. There was an unspoken war within her—torn between the intoxicating pull of Dorothy's presence and the safety of retreating into the familiar. The air around them felt alive, electric, charged with unfulfilled potential.

"And what would we talk about in private?" Elodie asked, her voice faint, almost trembling. But her gaze held steady, daring Dorothy to answer.

Dorothy leaned in closer, her lips a breath away from Elodie's ear, the scent of her faint perfume mingling with the heady musk of wine and stone. "Anything you want," she whispered, her voice curling like smoke. "Or nothing at all."

For a moment, Elodie was silent, her eyes flicking to Dorothy's lips before dropping to the space where their hands barely touched. Her hesitation was palpable, the weight of the decision she knew she was about to make pressing down on her chest.

"Lead the way," Elodie finally said, her voice barely audible but resolute.

Dorothy's lips quirked into a small, triumphant smile. Her fingers slid away from Elodie's wrist as she stood, the subtle scrape of her chair against the stone floor the only sound. Without another word, she gestured toward the dim hallway, her movements deliberate, confident.

Elodie followed, her steps uncertain but unrelenting. The shadows swallowed them as they left the room, leaving Edward engrossed in his sketch, unaware of the storm that had just passed —or perhaps, just begun.

Elodie's eyes darkened with something unspoken as she nodded, her fingers trembling slightly as they intertwined with Dorothy's. Together, they slipped away quietly, leaving Edward engrossed in his artistic fervor. The corridor stretched before them, dim and inviting, the shadows seeming to beckon them closer.

Dorothy stopped abruptly, turning to face Elodie. Without a word, she pressed her gently against the cool stone wall, their bodies flush. For a moment, she hesitated, her gaze searching Elodie's face as if seeking permission, confirmation, or perhaps a reflection of the same hunger that burned inside her.

"I've been wanting to do this all night," Dorothy whispered, her voice low and rough with need.

Elodie's lips parted as Dorothy leaned in, capturing them in a kiss that was slow yet searing, a deliberate exploration of sensation. The first brush of their mouths was tender, tentative, but quickly gave way to a deeper urgency. Elodie's hands rose instinctively, her fingers threading through Dorothy's hair, pulling her closer.

Dorothy's hands found Elodie's waist, her touch firm yet reverent as though she was both staking a claim and worshiping something sacred. The soft fabric of Elodie's dress slipped under Dorothy's fingertips, and she felt the rapid rise and fall of her chest, the unmistakable evidence of shared longing.

The kiss deepened, their breaths mingling, their movements becoming more insistent. Dorothy tilted her head, her lips traveling to the delicate line of Elodie's jaw, then lower to the curve of her neck. The faint scent of Elodie's perfume mixed with the musky warmth of their closeness, intoxicating and grounding all at once.

Elodie's fingers tightened in Dorothy's hair as a soft gasp escaped her lips. "Dorothy..." she breathed, her voice barely audible but heavy with emotion.

Dorothy pulled back slightly, just enough to look into Elodie's eyes. What she saw there—a blend of vulnerability, desire, and something deeper—sent a shiver through her. This wasn't just lust. It was connection, raw and unguarded, the kind that left you changed.

"You're incredible," Dorothy murmured, her forehead resting against Elodie's for a brief moment. "Do you know that?"

Elodie's response was to pull Dorothy back to her, their lips meeting again in a kiss that felt more like a conversation, each movement conveying what words could not. Dorothy's hands roamed with careful reverence, exploring the curve of Elodie's back, her sides, the elegant lines of her body as though committing them to memory.

The world outside faded. The distant murmurs from the main room, the creak of the manor's old floorboards—all of it became background noise, insignificant compared to the symphony of whispered breaths and quickened heartbeats.

Time seemed to stretch and condense simultaneously, their movements a delicate balance of urgency and restraint. As they clung to each other, Dorothy felt something shift within her, as though the moment had unearthed parts of herself she hadn't known existed.

When they finally pulled apart, their foreheads still touching, Dorothy could barely catch her breath. Elodie's hand rose to touch Dorothy's cheek, her thumb brushing softly against her skin.

"You surprise me," Elodie said, her voice trembling but sure. "And I don't know whether to run from that or embrace it."

Dorothy smiled, her own voice soft but steady. "Maybe you don't have to decide just yet."

They lingered there, the intimacy between them not fully spoken but deeply felt. In the quiet moments that followed, Dorothy realized this was more than an impulsive act—it was the beginning of something she wasn't sure she could name, but one she wasn't ready to let go of.

Later, as they lay tangled together in the dim light, Elodie's voice was husky as she leaned closer, her lips brushing Dorothy's ear. "You should come to London. There's so much more I'd like to show you."

Dorothy met her gaze, the weight of the words sinking in. This was more than an invitation—it was a challenge. "London?" she mused, a slow smile spreading across her face. "Now that could be interesting."

"Edward and I have a flat in Shoreditch," Elodie continued, her fingers tracing idle patterns on Dorothy's skin. "It's a different world from this quiet countryside. I think you'd like it."

Dorothy's mind raced with possibilities. London's vibrant energy, its blend of history and modernity, called to her adventurous spirit. And the promise of further exploration with Elodie…

"I just might take you up on that offer," Dorothy replied, her tone playful yet tinged with genuine intrigue.

๛

As Dorothy settled into bed that night, the scent of jasmine and Elodie's perfume still lingering on her skin, she let her thoughts drift. The glow of the bedside lamp cast long shadows across the room, elongating the quiet moments of reflection.

London. Elodie's words had planted a seed, one that had been slowly taking root ever since they met. Dorothy could see the city in her mind's eye—the glint of rain on cobblestones, the hum of its restless streets. She smiled faintly, a mix of curiosity and caution warring within her.

Her grandfather Émile's voice, as she'd imagined it, echoed in her mind: *"Opportunities come in whispers, my dear. It's up to you to answer."* Dorothy sighed, running a hand over the soft duvet.

Edward's laughter floated in from the common area, mingling with Elodie's lighter, knowing tone. Their easy camaraderie struck a chord deep within Dorothy, though she couldn't decide if it was harmony or dissonance.

"We'll see," she whispered to herself, the decision still distant on her horizon. For now, the promise of possibility was enough.

She turned off the lamp, letting the quiet of the night envelop her. Somewhere out there, life was waiting—but she wasn't ready to rush toward it just yet.

CHAPTER 5 – LONDON CALLING

Three months had passed since that sultry evening in the south of France, but the memory of it still lingered in Dorothy's mind like the scent of jasmine after a storm. Life in Paris had carried on, as it always did—columns to write, gallery openings to attend, and fleeting encounters that never quite scratched the itch of her restless soul.

But Elodie's invitation to London had refused to fade. At first, it had been an idle thought, something to revisit on lonely evenings. Then it became a spark, igniting her curiosity every time she saw Elodie's name pop up in her inbox or Edward sent her a sketch of a new piece inspired by their time together.

Now, standing on a rain-slicked cobblestone street in the heart of Shoreditch, Dorothy felt the weight of that decision. The city's pulse hit her immediately—taxi horns blared, neon lights reflected in puddles, and the damp air carried a mix of diesel fumes and fried food. Her nostrils flared, drinking in London's heady cocktail.

"Well, aren't you a beast," she murmured, her lips curving into a smile as she adjusted the strap of her emerald dress, the fabric shimmering under the soft glow of street lamps.

Three months ago, this had been a distant dream. Now, it was her reality.

Her heels clicked against the pavement with an assertive rhythm, each step claiming her place amidst the chaos. As she approached the gallery, Dorothy paused to adjust her fitted emerald dress, the fabric shimmering under the soft glow of street lamps.

Inside, heads turned as she swept through the room. Her laughter, rich and unguarded, drew people closer like moths to a flame. Dorothy reveled in the attention, her fingers trailing along the stem of her champagne flute.

"I don't believe we've met," a silver-haired man in a tailored suit said, sidling up to her. "I'm Charles."

Dorothy allowed her gaze to graze over him, a slow, deliberate perusal. "Dorothy," she purred, extending her hand. "Charmed, I'm sure."

Charles visibly swallowed, his eyes fixed on where their hands met. "The pleasure is mine. What brings you to our little soirée?"

"Oh, you know," Dorothy said airily, "art, intrigue, the promise of stimulating conversation." She leaned in closer, lowering her voice. "Though I must say, the company is proving far more enticing than the paintings."

Charles flushed, fumbling with his own champagne glass. Dorothy bit back a smile, relishing the effect she had on him. This was a dance she knew well, the delicate push and pull of attraction.

As Charles stammered through a response, Dorothy's mind wandered. How many nights like this had she experienced? Each city offered its own flavor of desire, its own cast of characters eager to be swept up in her orbit. And yet, beneath the familiar thrill, a whisper of restlessness stirred.

"I couldn't help but notice your interest in the Hartley piece," Charles said, gesturing to a nearby sculpture. "What are your thoughts?"

Dorothy cocked her head, considering. "It's... provocative," she said finally. "The way the light catches those jagged edges, don't you think? Beauty and danger, intertwined."

She felt a flicker of surprise at her own words. When had art started to mirror her inner landscape so acutely?

"Fascinating perspective," Charles murmured, leaning closer. "I'd love to hear more about your... interpretations."

Dorothy laughed, the sound both invitation and deflection. "Oh darling," she said, patting his arm, "I'm afraid that would take all night. And where's the mystery in that?"

As she moved away, melting into the crowd, Dorothy felt the familiar rush of power. She was the author of her own story here, weaving connections and severing them at will. And yet, as she caught her reflection in a polished sculpture, a question surfaced:

In a city of millions, in a world of endless possibility, why did she suddenly feel so achingly alone?

Dorothy's gaze lingered on the sculpture, its twisted metal and fractured glass an intricate dance of chaos and beauty. She stepped closer, drawn by an inexplicable pull. The gallery's soft lighting caught the edges, transforming harsh angles into something mesmerizing.

"It's like looking into a mirror," she murmured, her fingertips hovering just shy of the sculpture's surface.

A voice beside her broke through her reverie. "I couldn't agree more. It's captivating, isn't it?"

Dorothy turned, finding herself face-to-face with a woman whose eyes held a spark of genuine curiosity. She offered a slow, appraising smile.

"The artist seems to suggest chaos as a necessary prelude to creation, don't you think?" Dorothy tilted her head, a teasing lilt in her voice.

The woman leaned in, clearly spellbound. "Chaos, perhaps. Or reinvention?"

Dorothy's smile deepened. "Now you're speaking my language." She extended her hand. "Dorothy Duval."

"Evelyn Ashworth," the woman replied, her grip firm. "I must say, your insights are refreshing. Most here are more interested in the price tag than the art itself."

Dorothy laughed, a rich sound that drew eyes from across the room. "Oh darling, the true value of art lies in how it makes us feel, how it challenges us." She paused, considering. "Tell me, Evelyn, what does this piece awaken in you?"

As Evelyn began to speak, Dorothy found herself genuinely intrigued. Here was a mind as sharp as her own, a worthy sparring partner in this game of intellectual seduction. And yet, beneath the familiar thrill of connection, a new sensation stirred – a hunger for something beyond the fleeting encounters that had defined her life.

Is this what I've been searching for? Dorothy wondered, her eyes never leaving Evelyn's animated face. *A mirror that reflects more than just my own desires?*

The gallery's chatter faded to a dull murmur as Dorothy stepped out into the cool London night. Her mind buzzed with the evening's conversations, Evelyn's words echoing in her thoughts. She inhaled deeply, the crisp air a stark contrast to the warmth of champagne still lingering on her tongue.

"Green Park," she murmured to herself, drawn by an inexplicable urge to lose herself in nature's embrace. Her heels clicked a staccato rhythm on the pavement as she made her way towards the park's entrance.

The moment she stepped beneath the canopy of ancient oaks, a palpable shift occurred. The city's chaos receded, replaced by a primal stillness that sent a shiver down Dorothy's spine. She closed her eyes, inhaling deeply.

"God, this scent," she whispered, her voice husky. The earthy aroma of damp soil mingled with a faint trace of cologne – perhaps from a jogger who had passed moments before. It was an intoxicating mix that heightened her awareness of the city's hidden depths.

Dorothy's fingers trailed along the rough bark of a tree as she walked. "You've seen so much, haven't you?" she mused aloud. "If only these leaves could whisper their secrets."

A gust of wind rustled the branches, and for a moment, Dorothy could almost imagine the trees were answering her. She laughed softly at her own fanciful thoughts.

Is this what London does to a girl? she wondered. *Or is it just me, finally allowing myself to feel... something real?*

Her reverie was shattered by a sudden movement in her peripheral vision. Before Dorothy could react, a shadow materialized from the bushes. She barely had time to gasp before a hand clamped around her wrist, another yanking at her purse.

"No!" The word tore from her throat, primal and raw. Dorothy's free hand instinctively balled into a fist, but then she froze. The streetlight caught the glint of a blade, cold and unforgiving.

This can't be happening, her mind screamed, even as her body went limp with shock.

A rough shove sent her sprawling to the ground. The impact scraped her knees through her stockings, tearing delicate fabric and soft skin alike. But it was the sting of humiliation that cut deepest, far sharper than any physical pain.

As quickly as it began, it was over. Footsteps pounded away, leaving Dorothy alone with the lingering scent of fear and violated trust.

Dorothy stumbled down the rain-slicked street, her chest heaving with ragged breaths. The world around her spun, the bright neon lights of Shoreditch blurring into smudges of color against the encroaching darkness. Her hands clutched her bag tightly to her chest, the mugger hadn't managed to rip from her grasp.

"Are you okay?" A passerby slowed, concern flickering across their face. Dorothy tried to answer, but her voice failed her. She waved them off, unwilling to explain, unwilling to admit the vulnerability she felt crawling beneath her skin.

Her heels clicked unevenly on the pavement as she fought to regain composure. *Keep walking. You're fine. It's just a bad night,* she told herself. But the trembling in her hands and the tear in her dress betrayed the lie.

The golden glow of a familiar doorway appeared ahead—her hotel, a boutique retreat she'd chosen for its understated charm. Relief surged through her as the doorman caught sight of her.

"Madame Duval!" he greeted, his expression shifting immediately as he noticed her disheveled state. "Are you alright? Shall I fetch someone?"

Dorothy shook her head, forcing a smile she didn't feel. "I'm fine, André," she murmured, her accent more clipped than usual. "Just… send up a pot of tea, would you?"

André hesitated, clearly unconvinced, but nodded. "Of course, madame. Right away."

She stepped into the sleek marble lobby, its warmth and tranquility a stark contrast to the chaos outside. Her stilettos left faint wet marks on the polished floor as she crossed to the lift, her eyes avoiding her reflection in the mirrored walls.

Once inside her room, Dorothy locked the door behind her and sagged against it, exhaling shakily. The room was just as she'd left it that morning: immaculate, with crisp white sheets and the faint scent of lavender from the linen spray.

She dropped her bag onto the bed and kicked off her shoes, her hands still trembling. Crossing to the en suite, she stared at herself in the mirror. Mascara had smeared beneath her eyes, giving her an almost feral look. The tear in her dress revealed a graze on her knee where she'd fallen during the attack.

Her lips trembled, but no tears came. Dorothy reached for a makeup wipe, her movements precise as she began to clean the smudges from her face. The ritual steadied her, each swipe of the cloth a reclaiming of control.

"You won't win," she whispered to the memory of the mugger, her voice low but firm. Her reflection met her gaze, and she straightened her shoulders.

After slipping into a silk robe, Dorothy sank onto the bed and pulled out her phone. The temptation to call someone—to tell them what had happened—flickered briefly before she dismissed it. Instead, she typed out a note in her digital diary app, the words flowing like a release:

"Shoreditch isn't as charming as I'd hoped tonight. But I'll be damned if I let one coward ruin it for me."

As the tea arrived, Dorothy sipped it slowly, her mind already crafting the next chapter of her London adventure. Tonight had been a misstep, but it wouldn't define her. It was just another story in a city full of them.

※

Dorothy reached for the teapot, her hands steady now, though her body still hummed with the evening's chaos. She poured the steaming liquid into her delicate porcelain cup, the scent of jasmine rising to meet her. Her gaze drifted to the mini-bar, and with a hint of a smile, she grabbed the small bottle of brandy.

"A little extra courage," she murmured, tipping a generous splash into her tea. The golden liquid swirled, deepening the aroma. She raised the cup to her lips, the warmth soothing her even as the brandy ignited a slow burn in her chest.

Leaning back against the plush armchair, Dorothy allowed the silk robe to slip slightly, exposing her collarbone. Her fingertips grazed the edge of the fabric, tracing the curve of her neck, then lower, skimming the swell of her breast. Each touch was deliberate, a silent reclaiming of her body after the invasion of the evening.

Her reflection in the mirror caught her attention, and she turned to face it fully. The candlelight from the bedside table cast a golden hue on her skin, accentuating the glimmer of vulnerability in her eyes. She stepped closer, setting her tea aside, her hands moving with an unhurried sensuality.

Fingertips brushed over the delicate bruises on her shoulder, then wandered lower, her palms grazing her ribs, her stomach. There was an undeniable power in the way she explored herself—not in shame, but in reverence. "You're still here," she whispered to her reflection, her voice low and breathless. "You're still… magnificent."

Her hand hovered at her waist, slipping beneath the silk, the sensation of the fabric against her skin both tantalizing and grounding. A faint blush rose to her cheeks as she allowed herself to let go, her body responding to the rhythm of her touch, her eyes locked with her reflection.

The room seemed to hold its breath, her gasps soft but deliberate, a symphony of release and rediscovery. As her body shuddered, her lips parted in a sigh, and she leaned against the edge of the vanity, her head tilting back.

Moments later, Dorothy stood straighter, her cheeks flushed, her breath evening out. She caught her reflection once more, this time smiling faintly. The tear tracks from earlier had dried, leaving only a faint shimmer on her cheekbones.

"Vulnerability," she murmured, her voice now laced with satisfaction, "isn't weakness. It's... creation."

She reached for her tea, the brandy-infused warmth a perfect complement to her renewed sense of self. Raising the cup in a private toast, she locked eyes with her reflection one last time. "To reinvention," she declared. "And to never apologizing for it."

🦢

Dorothy awoke to the pale light of dawn filtering through the hotel curtains. The silk robe she had wrapped herself in the night before was now discarded on the edge of the bed, a remnant of her evening of reflection. Stretching slowly, she sat up, her body aching faintly but her mind sharp and clear. The previous evening's bruises, both literal and emotional, felt like distant memories now—still present but dulled, like shadows retreating with the morning sun.

Swinging her legs over the side of the bed, Dorothy's toes met the plush carpet as she reached for the glass of water she'd placed on the bedside table. The faint hum of London traffic outside reminded her of where she was, and more importantly, where she was headed.

"No more dwelling," she murmured to herself, setting the empty glass aside and rising to her feet.

Her suitcase sat open on the bench at the foot of the bed, its contents neatly arranged despite the chaos of the past day. Dorothy's gaze fell on a black dress she'd packed as a failsafe—a classic, understated piece that radiated quiet confidence. She picked it up, running her fingers over the smooth fabric. *Perfect.*

In the bathroom, the steam from a quick shower fogged the mirror as she prepared herself. The dark circles under her eyes from a restless night had softened, her skin glowing faintly from the cool water. Dorothy applied her makeup with the precision of an artist, her bold red lipstick the final touch—a pop of defiance against the city that had tried to shake her.

The black dress fit her like armor, its elegant simplicity a sharp contrast to the glimmering emerald gown from the previous evening. As she zipped it up, Dorothy felt a shift within herself, a return to the poised and fearless woman she knew she could be.

Grabbing her coat and bag, Dorothy hesitated at the door, her hand hovering over the brass handle. She glanced back at the room, its minimalist décor now a backdrop for her resurgence. With a deep breath, she stepped into the corridor, her heels clicking rhythmically against the marble floor.

The lobby was bustling with early risers—travelers checking out, businesspeople on their phones. Dorothy caught her reflection in the gilded mirror near the entrance. The woman staring back was someone she recognized: focused, determined, and undeniably alluring.

She smirked, tilting her chin upward. "London," she whispered, her voice low and confident, "you may have knocked me down, but now it's my turn."

Pushing through the revolving doors, Dorothy emerged into the brisk morning air. The city sprawled before her, its energy palpable. The golden light bathed the streets, and Dorothy strode forward with purpose, each step echoing her intent.

The black dress swayed as she walked, her coat cinched tight against the chill. London had shown its teeth, but Dorothy thrived on challenge. She was no stranger to taming wild beasts, and this city was no exception.

Her lips curved into a sly smile. "Let's see what you've got," she murmured, her heels clicking a deliberate rhythm as she disappeared into the labyrinth of London's possibilities.

CHAPTER 6 – UNEXPECTED REVELATIONS

Dorothy Duval's stiletto heels clicked rhythmically on the hardwood floor, her arrival at the eclectic London townhouse announcing itself like a line of poetry in a sea of prose. The space was a cacophony of color and texture, with abstract canvases adorning the walls like a choir of visual sirens. Velvet drapes pooled like spilled wine, and the heady scent of cedar and sandalwood wove an intoxicating tapestry in the air. Each detail—from the mismatched furniture to the scattered paintbrushes—spoke of a curated chaos, a perfect reflection of its bohemian inhabitants.

Edward, the paint-flecked artist she'd met on her way to Cannes, stood amidst the organized chaos, his eyes alight with the same intensity that had captured her attention across the gallery floor. "Dorothy! I'm so glad you could join us," he said, enveloping her in a warm hug. But it was the woman behind him—the enigmatic Elodie—who captivated her.

Elodie's silk blouse caressed her slender form, slipping just off one shoulder, as if even the fabric couldn't bear to fully conceal her porcelain skin. Her eyes held the faintest of smiles, their depths like the still waters of a hidden lagoon. "It's a pleasure to see you again," Elodie purred, her voice like honey dripping on forbidden fruit.

Dorothy felt the weight of Elodie's gaze, a quiet intensity that seemed to see right through her Parisian facade. Surrounded by the vibrancy of the townhouse, she suddenly felt like a single brushstroke on a canvas yearning for more color. Her usual composure, so effortlessly maintained, frayed ever so slightly in the face of Elodie's unguarded confidence.

As they sat down to lunch, the three of them weaved a tapestry of conversation, their voices intertwining like the strands of a Ravel composition. Edward spoke of his latest inspirations, his words as fluid as his brushstrokes, while Elodie listened with an attentive ear and a knowing smile. Dorothy found herself drawn to the enigmatic woman, her own carefully cultivated flirtations daring to venture into uncharted territory.

Over the course of the meal, the wine flowed like a river through their veins, loosening inhibitions and loyalties alike. The air between them grew thick with unspoken promises, and as dessert was cleared away, Dorothy couldn't help but wonder if this was the beginning of something altogether more delicious than she could have ever anticipated.

The air in the room shifted as Edward burst through the doorway, his presence as vibrant as the splashes of cobalt blue dotting his shirt. His eyes, a startling azure, locked onto Dorothy with an intensity that sent a ripple of excitement through her.

"Dorothy!" Edward exclaimed, his voice rich with warmth. "You're a vision in this chaos we call home."

Dorothy felt his gaze linger on the curve of her neck, tracing a line that made her skin tingle. She tilted her head slightly, a calculated move that exposed more of her collarbone. "Edward," she purred, "your home is a masterpiece. Much like its creator."

His cheeks flushed, matching the passionate red of a nearby canvas. "You flatter me," he said, running a paint-stained hand through his disheveled hair. "I've been working on a new series. Would you like to hear about it?"

Dorothy nodded, her eyes never leaving his. "I'd love nothing more."

As Edward launched into a fervent description of his latest work, Dorothy let her mind wander. She's always enjoyed the way his passion consumed him, how he seemed to forget the world when he spoke of art. It made him... pliable.

"It's about the interplay of light and shadow," Edward was saying, his hands painting invisible strokes in the air. "The way darkness can define brightness, how absence can make presence more profound."

"Fascinating," Dorothy murmured, deliberately brushing her arm against his as she leaned in. "It sounds like you're exploring more than just paint on canvas."

Edward's breath caught, and Dorothy suppressed a smile. Too easy, she thought.

Their moment was interrupted by Elodie's melodic voice. "Edward, darling, why don't you fetch us some more wine from the cellar while Dorothy and I chat?"

As Edward moved away, looking slightly dazed, Elodie turned to Dorothy with a knowing smile. "So, tell me about your travels. I hear you have quite the eye for beauty."

Dorothy felt a thrill at the double entendre. "Beauty comes in many forms," she replied, her gaze sweeping over Elodie's lithe form. "I find it's often in the unexpected places."

Elodie's eyes sparkled. "Speaking of unexpected, let me tell you about my latest painting. It's been... consuming me."

As Elodie described her work, her hands moved with a fluid grace that mesmerized Dorothy. She found herself leaning in, drawn by the passion in Elodie's voice.

"It's about tension and release," Elodie said, her fingers grazing Dorothy's wrist. The touch sent a jolt through her, unexpected and electric.

Dorothy's lips curved into a smile, her voice dropping to a low purr. "I know a little something about that."

Their eyes met, and for a moment, the air between them crackled with possibility. Dorothy felt her pulse quicken, a familiar heat blooming in her core. This, she thought, this is why I came here tonight.

❧

The sound of Edward clearing his throat broke the spell, drawing both women's attention. "I thought I'd give Dorothy the full tour before the light fades," he said, his tone light but his eyes flicking to Elodie, as if gauging her reaction.

Elodie's gaze lingered on Dorothy, her lips curving into a knowing smile. "Of course. Don't let me keep you." She stepped back gracefully, though her eyes seemed to hold an unspoken promise. "But don't forget to see the upstairs gallery—it's Edward's pride and joy."

Dorothy hesitated, caught between the magnetic pull of Elodie and the curiosity Edward was so eager to stoke. Finally, she nodded. "Lead the way," she said to Edward, though her thoughts lingered on Elodie's touch.

As they ascended the sweeping staircase, Dorothy could feel Edward's hand resting lightly on the small of her back. It was a touch she recognized—possessive, though not entirely unwelcome. His enthusiasm spilled over as he gestured at the eclectic array of artwork adorning the walls.

"And this," Edward said, stopping before a twisted metal sculpture, "is a piece I acquired in Berlin. The artist was exploring the concept of metamorphosis and—"

Dorothy leaned in closer, ostensibly to examine the artwork, but acutely aware of how her proximity affected Edward. His words faltered, trailing off into silence as her perfume enveloped him.

"Go on," she murmured, her breath warm against his ear. "You were saying something about metamorphosis?"

Edward swallowed hard, his Adam's apple bobbing. "I... yes, the transformation of—"

The sharp click of boots on hardwood interrupted him, drawing their attention to the doorway. Dorothy turned to see a striking woman with fiery red hair stride into the room, her presence commanding the space effortlessly. Dorothy felt a thrill of anticipation course through her.

"Joan," Edward said, a hint of relief in his voice. "You're here. Perfect timing."

Joan's green eyes settled on Dorothy, curiosity and challenge mingling in her gaze. "So," she said, extending a hand, "you must be the famous Dorothy."

Dorothy met Joan's grip firmly, relishing the subtle test of dominance in the handshake. "I've heard a lot about you too," she replied, arching a brow. "All good, I hope."

A smirk played at the corner of Joan's lips. "Now where's the fun in that?"

Dorothy couldn't suppress a grin. This woman was different—direct, unapologetic. She found herself intrigued by the thought of peeling back Joan's layers.

Edward, sensing the shift in energy, interjected eagerly. "I was just showing Dorothy our collection," he said, gesturing toward the walls.

Joan's gaze flicked to Edward, then back to Dorothy. "And how are you finding our little menagerie of oddities?"

"Fascinating," Dorothy purred, her eyes never leaving Joan's. "Though I suspect the most intriguing pieces aren't hanging on the walls."

Joan's smirk widened into a genuine smile. "Perceptive. I think you'll fit in just fine here, Dorothy."

As Joan moved further into the room, Dorothy caught herself admiring the sway of her hips, the confident set of her shoulders. She felt a familiar hunger stirring within her—the desire to explore, to unravel, to consume. This afternoon, she realized, had just become infinitely more interesting.

The living room hummed with anticipation as Edward clapped his hands together, his eyes bright with excitement. "I've just had a brilliant idea," he announced, his gaze flitting between the assembled faces. "Let's have an impromptu dinner party!"

Dorothy leaned back against the plush velvet of the sofa, crossing her legs as she observed the others' reactions. Elodie, seated beside her, shared a glance, her lips curving into a warm, indulgent smile. "Edward, darling," Elodie said with a teasing lilt, "do you even know what's in the pantry? Or are you planning to conjure a feast out of thin air?"

"Spontaneity suits you, Edward," Dorothy remarked, her voice a low purr. "Though I hope you're as skilled in the kitchen as you are with a paintbrush."

Edward's cheeks flushed, pleasure and nervousness mingling in his expression. "Oh, I have a few culinary tricks up my sleeve."

"I'll believe it when I see it," Elodie quipped, her gaze dancing between Edward and Dorothy. "But don't think you're getting off without help. Dinner parties are a group effort."

As Edward bustled off to the kitchen, Joan, who had been lounging in an armchair across from Dorothy, leaned forward slightly, her green eyes glinting with curiosity. "So, Dorothy," she began, her tone casual but her gaze sharp. "What brings a Parisian sophisticate like yourself to our humble London abode?"

Dorothy chuckled, the sound rich and velvety. "Humble? Hardly. But let's just say I have a weakness for... interesting company." She cast a deliberate glance between Joan and Elodie, the latter arching an amused brow at the implicit compliment.

"And what qualifies as interesting in your book?" Joan pressed, leaning closer.

Dorothy's pulse quickened at the proximity, though she was keenly aware of Elodie's presence beside her. "Oh, you know. People who aren't afraid to push boundaries, to question the status quo."

"Is that what you're doing here? Pushing boundaries?" Joan's question hung in the air, loaded with implication.

Dorothy felt a thrill run through her, the kind she lived for. She let the corner of her mouth quirk into a knowing smile. "I believe in exploring all life has to offer," she replied, her voice dropping to a near-whisper. "The light and the dark, the sacred and the profane. After all, isn't that what makes us truly alive?"

Elodie, who had been quietly observing, leaned back and crossed her legs with deliberate grace. "Exploration is one thing," she said softly, her tone thoughtful. "But knowing when to dive deeper... that's where the real challenge lies, don't you think?"

Joan's lips curved into a slow smile, her gaze flicking briefly to Elodie before settling back on Dorothy. "I don't believe in good or bad. Only interesting."

The words struck Dorothy like a match to kindling, igniting something deep within her. She found herself reassessing her initial impressions of both Joan and Elodie, intrigued by the layers of complexity beneath their exteriors.

"And what do you find interesting, Joan?" Dorothy asked, her curiosity piqued.

Before Joan could respond, Edward's voice called out from the kitchen, breaking the moment. "Ladies, could I get a hand with the hors d'oeuvres? And someone check the wine rack—I might have gone a bit overboard uncorking bottles."

Dorothy rose gracefully, extending a hand to Joan. "Shall we? I'm dying to see what culinary delights await us."

Elodie stood as well, smoothing her skirt with effortless poise. "Let's not leave him to his own devices. Last time he hosted, we had three kinds of soup and nothing else."

As they moved toward the kitchen, the dynamic between the three women pulsed with a subtle tension. Dorothy couldn't shake the feeling that this evening was about to take an unexpected, thrilling turn. The boundaries of her desires were already blurring, and the night had only just begun.

The dining room glowed with an intimate warmth as candles flickered along the table, their golden light dancing across half-filled wine glasses and tangled silverware. Dorothy settled into her chair, inhaling the rich aroma of herbs and spices that wafted from the kitchen. The hum of conversation buzzed around her like an electric current, every glance charged with unspoken truths.

"I hope everyone's hungry," Edward announced, setting down a platter of roasted vegetables. His eyes found Dorothy's, lingering a moment too long. "I may have gone a bit overboard."

Dorothy smiled, her voice teasing. "Is that even possible for an artist? I thought excess was part of the job description."

Edward laughed, a hint of color rising to his cheeks. "You've got me there. Though I prefer to think of it as... passionate enthusiasm."

As the meal progressed, Dorothy found herself acutely aware of Edward's gaze. It returned to her frequently, growing more heated with each glass of wine. His words became increasingly effusive, punctuated by grand gestures that sent droplets of red flying from his glass.

"Dorothy," he exclaimed, leaning in conspiratorially, "you simply must let me paint you someday. There's something about the way the light catches your skin... it's positively luminous."

She let him look, the corner of her mouth curling in quiet amusement. "Careful, Edward," she purred. "A girl might get ideas with that kind of talk."

Inwardly, Dorothy's mind raced. She'd known Edward was attracted to her, but this open display was unexpected. It added another layer of complexity to the evening's dynamics, one she found both flattering and potentially useful.

A lull in conversation drew her attention across the table. In the momentary quiet, she caught a subtle exchange between Elodie and Joan. Dorothy's breath caught as she saw Elodie's fingers brush Joan's thigh under the table, the movement as intimate as a whisper. The way Joan leaned into the touch, her eyes fluttering closed for a fraction of a second, was electric.

Dorothy blinked, surprised by the depth of connection evident in that fleeting moment. She'd sensed an easy familiarity between the two women earlier, but this... this spoke of something far more profound.

"More wine, Dorothy?" Elodie's voice startled her from her observations.

"Please," Dorothy replied, holding out her glass. As Elodie poured, their eyes met, and Dorothy wondered if her witnessing of that tender moment had been noticed. "This is a lovely vintage. You have excellent taste."

Elodie's smile was enigmatic. "In wine, and in company, I'd like to think."

Dorothy raised her glass in a small toast. "I'll drink to that."

As she sipped, Dorothy's mind whirled with the possibilities unfolding before her. The evening had taken on a charged, sensual energy that thrilled her. Every interaction felt laden with potential, and she found herself eager to see where the night might lead.

The candles had burned low, their flickering light casting long shadows across the now-empty plates. Edward leaned back in his chair, his artistic fingers idly tracing the rim of his wine glass.

"You know," he said, his gaze drifting between Dorothy and Joan, "I've always admired the honesty in Elodie and Joan's relationship. It's refreshing, really."

Dorothy's eyebrows arched slightly. "Oh?" she prompted, her curiosity piqued.

Edward nodded, a lazy smile playing on his lips. "They've been together for years now. Open about it, too. It's quite beautiful to witness."

The casual revelation sent a jolt through Dorothy's system. She'd suspected, of course, after witnessing their intimate moment, but hearing it stated so plainly added a new dimension to the evening's dynamics.

"I see," Dorothy murmured, her gaze flicking to Joan, who met her eyes with an unwavering intensity. "And you're... comfortable with that arrangement?"

Edward chuckled, oblivious to the charged undercurrent between the two women. "Why wouldn't I be? Love is love, in all its forms."

As the group began to disperse, Dorothy found herself gravitating towards Joan, drawn by an inexorable pull of attraction and curiosity. They ended up on the balcony, the cool night air a stark contrast to the heat building between them.

Joan leaned against the railing, her red hair catching the moonlight. "So, what do you make of our little ménage, Dorothy?"

Dorothy's pulse quickened at Joan's directness. "It's... intriguing," she admitted. "I've always found traditional boundaries to be rather limiting."

"Hmm," Joan hummed, stepping closer. The heat of her body radiated against Dorothy's skin. "You like control, don't you?" she murmured, her lips hovering near Dorothy's ear.

Dorothy smirked, her voice a purr. "Only when it's worth taking."

Joan's fingers traced the curve of Dorothy's jaw, her touch deliberate and unhurried. Dorothy leaned in, their lips brushing like a promise before deepening into something far more explicit.

As they kissed, Dorothy's mind raced. This was dangerous territory, she knew. But the thrill of it, the raw honesty of desire – it was intoxicating. She pulled back slightly, breathless.

"What about Elodie?" she whispered, a last thread of hesitation.

Joan's green eyes sparkled with mischief. "What about her? She knows exactly where I am, Dorothy. The question is, do you know where you are?"

Dorothy swallowed hard, realizing she was on the precipice of something both exhilarating and potentially life-altering. Joan's hand, warm and steady, rested lightly on her forearm. The gesture seemed casual, but Dorothy felt its weight, its intention. She hesitated, her gaze flickering to the doorway as if Elodie might appear at any moment, but she found herself drawn back to Joan's eyes, full of challenge and invitation.

"I think I do," Dorothy replied, her voice low, a tremor of anticipation lacing her words.

The tension snapped like a taut string, and Joan's lips met hers in a kiss that was fierce and unyielding. Dorothy's back hit the edge of the kitchen counter as Joan pressed closer, her hands sliding up Dorothy's sides, fingers grazing bare skin where her blouse had ridden up. Dorothy responded in kind, her hands tangling in Joan's fiery hair, pulling her closer still.

The kiss deepened, a clash of hunger and dominance. Joan's teeth grazed Dorothy's lower lip, eliciting a soft gasp. Dorothy arched into her, a thrill racing through her at the feeling of relinquishing control to this commanding presence. The room around them seemed to dissolve; there was only the heat of Joan's mouth, the press of her body, and the dizzying sensation of losing herself.

༺༻

Dorothy's fingers trailed along the silk sheets of her borrowed bed, the cool fabric a stark contrast to the heat still lingering on her skin. The distant hum of London traffic filtered through the open window, a rhythmic backdrop to her swirling thoughts.

She closed her eyes, Joan's husky voice echoing in her mind. "Do you know where you are?"

A wry smile played on Dorothy's lips. "Where indeed," she murmured to the empty room, her hand absently brushing the curve of her shoulder where Joan's lips had lingered.

The evening's memories replayed in her mind: Joan's deliberate touch, the strength in her embrace, the way she had guided Dorothy's body like a sculptor shaping clay. It had been exhilarating, primal, and entirely unlike anything Dorothy had experienced before. And yet, even amidst the intensity, there had been moments of surprising tenderness—a thumb brushing her cheek, a whispered word that felt like a promise.

Rolling onto her side, Dorothy reached for her phone, hesitating before opening her digital diary app. Her fingertips hovered over the screen, torn between the urge to document and the desire to simply let the evening's sensations wash over her.

"To hell with it," Dorothy muttered, beginning to type:

Tonight was... unexpected. Joan's touch still burns, but it's the web I've woven that truly fascinates me. Elodie's quiet intensity, like still waters running deep. Edward's yearning, so transparent yet endearing. And Joan... God, Joan's hunger matches my own.

She paused, considering her next words carefully. *Am I Émile's granddaughter after all? Playing with fire, dancing on the edge of propriety?*

A soft knock at the door interrupted her musings. Dorothy's heart leapt, equal parts anticipation and trepidation coursing through her veins.

"Yes?" she called out, her voice steadier than she felt.

The door creaked open, revealing Edward's tousled hair and paint-smudged t-shirt. His boyish smile faltered slightly as his gaze took in Dorothy sitting against the headboard, the sheet draped loosely around her.

"Sorry to disturb you," he said, his voice soft, his gaze flickering nervously. "I just wanted to make sure you were comfortable. And to say... well, to say that I hope tonight hasn't made things awkward."

Dorothy tilted her head, watching him with quiet amusement. "Awkward?" she echoed, arching an eyebrow. "My dear Edward, I think we've long passed the point of awkwardness, don't you?"

Edward's cheeks flushed a deep red, and Dorothy caught the slight hitch in his breath as her sheet slipped a fraction lower, revealing the curve of her collarbone. She held his gaze, her own lips curling into a slow, deliberate smile.

"Come here," she said, her voice low and commanding, and she was gratified by the way Edward obeyed without hesitation.

He approached the bed, tentative at first, until Dorothy reached out, her fingers curling around the hem of his t-shirt. She pulled him closer, her movements unhurried but deliberate. Edward sat on the edge of the bed, his hand brushing hers as if asking for permission.

"You're sweet," Dorothy murmured, her other hand trailing up his arm, tracing the muscles beneath the fabric. "But I don't need sweet tonight, Edward. I need real."

His response was a kiss—eager, tentative at first, but growing bolder as Dorothy guided him, her hands threading through his hair, pulling him down onto the bed with her. The weight of him was solid, grounding, and she relished the contrast between his nervous energy and the quiet confidence she felt enveloping them.

Their movements grew more urgent, Edward's hands exploring the curves of her body, his lips trailing down her neck. Dorothy arched beneath him, her nails grazing his back, coaxing him further. She felt the tension in his body, the restrained passion waiting to be unleashed, and she reveled in the power of drawing it out of him.

"Show me," Dorothy whispered against his ear, her voice a challenge and an invitation. And when he did, she found herself surprised by the depth of his intensity, the rawness of his desire.

As they lay tangled together in the aftermath, Edward's head resting against her shoulder, Dorothy traced idle patterns on his back. Her mind wandered to Joan, to Elodie, to the tangled web she was weaving, each thread pulling tighter around her.

The night stretched on, and Dorothy felt alive in a way she hadn't in years.

CHAPTER 7 – THE ART OF RETREAT

Mordecai took a deep breath as he entered the gallery, allowing the sensory overload to wash over him. The room teemed with vibrant artwork and an even more vibrant crowd. The scent of champagne mingled with the faint tang of varnish, and laughter rippled through the air like brushstrokes on a canvas. He knew tonight would unravel more than just artistic intentions.

The trip to London hadn't been planned. Just days ago, he'd been in Paris, comfortably ensconced in his atelier, when the call came. Not from Dorothy herself, but from Edward. The young artist's voice had trembled with urgency, weaving a story of confusion and unease.

"She's... different lately," Edward had confessed. "Brilliant as ever, but there's something off. She's pushing boundaries—hers and everyone else's. And Joan, she's furious. It's like a storm is brewing, and I don't know how to stop it."

Mordecai had listened carefully, his instincts stirring. Dorothy had always been a master at crafting chaos, but she was also adept at managing it—turning even her messiest moments into something artful. If Edward was this unsettled, something significant must have shifted.

"You want me to come to London?" Mordecai had asked, more to confirm his suspicions than out of genuine surprise.

Edward's reply had been immediate. "Yes. You're the only one she listens to."

The words had hung in the air, their weight undeniable. Mordecai had hesitated for only a moment before agreeing. Dorothy was many things—muse, enigma, and occasional tormentor—but above all, she was a friend. If she was teetering on the edge of something, he couldn't stand idly by.

And now here he was, in the heart of London's art scene, seeking answers that only Dorothy could provide.

※

Edward stood before his latest masterpiece, gesticulating with paint-stained hands as he explained the intricate brushwork to a small crowd of admirers. His voice was animated, but his eyes kept darting across the room to where Dorothy held court, the faintest trace of longing etched into his features.

"The interplay of light and shadow," Edward mused, his words faltering as Dorothy's melodic laughter cut through the air. He blinked, momentarily disoriented. "Ah, yes, the chiaroscuro effect here..." The crowd chuckled politely, their attention splitting between Edward's enthusiasm and the gravitational pull of Dorothy's presence.

Mordecai observed it all from a distance, leaning against a column as his sharp eyes tracked the room's currents. He saw the way Edward's gestures grew more erratic, his confidence wavering each time Dorothy moved or spoke. The young artist's admiration was painfully obvious, tinged with the kind of melancholy that came from unspoken desires. Mordecai wondered if Edward realized how his own brilliance dimmed in Dorothy's radiant wake—or if that was the price he was willing to pay for her attention.

A gravelly voice cut through Mordecai's thoughts. "Quite the spectacle, isn't it?"

Joan materialized at his side, her red hair a vivid contrast to the sleek black of her dress. She held a glass of whiskey, the amber liquid swirling lazily as her emerald eyes sharpened on the scene before them.

"Edward?" Mordecai asked lightly, already anticipating her response.

Joan snorted, the sound laced with exasperation. "Edward's infatuation is almost sweet. Almost. But he's not the real story, is he?" Her gaze drifted pointedly to Dorothy, who was effortlessly commanding the attention of another group. "It's her. It's always her."

"She does have a way of pulling people into her orbit," Mordecai acknowledged, his tone neutral. He could feel Joan's simmering anger, though she masked it well behind her sardonic smile.

"Pulling people in?" Joan's lips curled into a bitter smirk. "Try consuming them. Leaving them spent, hollowed out, and wondering why the world suddenly feels a little less bright."

Mordecai regarded her thoughtfully. "You're speaking from experience, I take it?"

Joan's expression darkened, and she took a long sip of whiskey before answering. "I've watched her do this too many times. To Edward. To Elodie. To me." Her voice dipped lower, edged with steel. "And the worst part? I don't even think she realizes the damage she causes. Or maybe she just doesn't care."

Mordecai tilted his head, considering Dorothy as she laughed, her champagne flute sparkling in her hand. "I think she notices everything. But caring? That's a question for Dorothy herself."

Joan's eyes narrowed. "Diplomatic as ever, Mordecai. But you and I both know she thrives on this chaos. It fuels her, just as much as it ruins the rest of us."

Before Mordecai could respond, Edward's voice rose above the crowd, trembling with excitement as he announced his next project—a series inspired by the "ephemeral beauty of modern goddesses." His eyes, alight with fervor, locked onto Dorothy's form, and his audience broke into polite applause.

Mordecai felt a twinge of something—concern? Fascination? As he watched Edward beam with pride, he couldn't shake the feeling that the young artist was setting himself up for a spectacular fall. "Perhaps," Mordecai murmured, turning back to Joan, "we're witnessing both inspiration and destruction tonight."

Joan's jaw tightened. "She's already got Edward dangling by a thread. And Elodie? She's barely here anymore. Have you noticed? Ever since Dorothy and Edward got closer, Elodie's withdrawn. The cracks are there, even if Dorothy pretends not to see them."

Mordecai frowned, glancing around. It was true—Elodie was absent from the immediate scene, and the thought troubled him. She was often the quiet balance to Dorothy's chaos, but now, her absence felt conspicuous.

"Where is she?" Mordecai asked, his voice soft but insistent.

Joan shrugged, her expression carefully blank. "Somewhere. Nursing her wounds, probably. Or trying to find a way to stay relevant in Dorothy's shadow. You know how this works, Mordecai. Dorothy doesn't share the spotlight."

As Dorothy began to make her way toward them, champagne

flute in hand and her satin dress shimmering under the gallery lights, Mordecai felt the tension coil tighter. Joan straightened, her emerald eyes narrowing in anticipation.

"Dorothy, darling," Joan drawled as she approached, her tone sharp despite the smile on her lips. "Come to dazzle us further, or simply to ensure no one forgets you're the star of the evening?"

Dorothy's laughter was light and musical, but Mordecai caught the flicker of something behind her eyes—irritation? Weariness? "Oh, Joan. Always so dramatic. I simply thought I'd say hello before the gossip became too juicy."

"And here I thought you thrived on gossip," Joan countered, her words laced with venom.

Mordecai stepped between them, his voice calm but firm. "Perhaps we should save the theatrics for another time. There's enough drama in the art, don't you think?"

Dorothy's gaze lingered on him, and for a moment, Mordecai thought he saw a flicker of vulnerability. But then her mask of confidence slid back into place, and she turned her attention to the crowd, leaving the unspoken tensions to simmer in her wake.

🦢

Dorothy glided towards them, her satin dress shimmering under the gallery lights, a champagne flute balanced delicately between her fingers. Her arrival sent ripples through the room, drawing eyes and murmurs in her wake. Mordecai noted how Edward's gaze instinctively tracked her, his fingers tightening around his glass as though bracing himself.

When Dorothy's eyes met Joan's, the temperature between them seemed to drop a degree, though the air thrummed with an electric undercurrent. A challenge sparkled in Joan's emerald gaze, sharp and unrelenting.

"Joan, darling," Dorothy began, her tone as light and effervescent as the champagne in her glass. "You look like you have something on your mind. Care to share with the class?"

Joan's lips curled into a smile that didn't quite reach her eyes. "Oh, you know me," she drawled, her voice smooth but tinged with venom. "Always observing. Though tonight, I find myself wondering how many lives you'll unravel before the evening is through."

The statement hung in the air like smoke, thick and acrid. Mordecai's gaze shifted between the two women, acutely aware of the tension coiling tighter with every second. Dorothy's laugh cut through the moment, melodic yet hollow.

"Oh, Joan," she said, shaking her head with a mock-playful sigh. "Always so dramatic. I prefer to think of it as... inspiring people to embrace their true selves."

"Is that what you call it?" Joan's voice dropped, low and edged with steel. "Inspiration? And what about Edward? Is he embracing his true self, or just chasing your shadow?"

Edward, who had been lingering nearby, froze at the mention of his name. His cheeks flushed, but he didn't move, as though rooted in place by the weight of Joan's accusation. Mordecai saw the young artist's gaze flicker nervously to Dorothy, seeking reassurance he would not find.

Dorothy's fingers tightened imperceptibly around her glass, the faintest crack in her polished veneer. For a fleeting moment, something flickered in her eyes—hesitation, perhaps even guilt—but it vanished as quickly as it had appeared, replaced by her usual mask of confidence.

"Edward is an artist," she replied, her voice steady, almost clinical. "He finds inspiration where he chooses. I'm merely a muse, nothing more."

Joan's sharp laugh cut through the air. "A muse with a rather impressive body count," she shot back, her green eyes flashing with something deeper—betrayal, perhaps, or a long-held grudge finally surfacing. "But I suppose that's the thing about muses. They inspire, but they also destroy."

Mordecai watched the interplay with a detached intensity, his mind racing to piece together the fractured history between these two women. There were layers here, years of shared experience and unspoken resentments bubbling beneath the surface. He could sense the depth of Joan's bitterness, and though Dorothy held her ground, the subtle tension in her posture betrayed her awareness of the truth in Joan's words.

As Dorothy opened her mouth to retort, Mordecai caught a fleeting expression cross her face—a mixture of defiance and something more vulnerable, more complex. It was a look that lingered for only a heartbeat, but it told him more than any words could. There were hidden currents beneath her dazzling exterior, threads of doubt and perhaps even regret woven into the fabric of her charm.

Mordecai stepped in, his voice calm and measured. "Perhaps this is a conversation better suited for somewhere less public," he suggested, his eyes locking briefly with Dorothy's. "Unless, of course, you're hoping to give the entire gallery something new to gossip about."

Dorothy's laugh returned, light and deliberate, though it didn't quite reach her eyes. "You're always the peacemaker, aren't you, Mordecai?" she said, her tone as smooth as silk. "But perhaps you're right. Joan and I do have a habit of making spectacles of ourselves."

Joan's smile was razor-sharp as she raised her glass in mock salute. "Only when the spectacle demands it," she replied.

Dorothy inclined her head, the motion almost imperceptible. Her gaze flicked to Edward, who still stood frozen at the edge of the confrontation, his expression a mix of awe and unease. Something in Dorothy's expression softened as she met his eyes —a moment of unspoken reassurance that only deepened the tension between her and Joan.

Mordecai stepped to Dorothy's side, his hand ghosting over her elbow in a gesture of quiet support. "Shall we find some fresh air?" he murmured, his voice low.

Dorothy nodded, allowing him to guide her away from the center of the room. But as they moved, Mordecai couldn't shake the feeling that the storm between Dorothy and Joan was far from over. And in its wake, it would leave more than just whispered gossip and shattered glasses—it would leave scars.

Joan watched them go, her emerald eyes dark and unreadable. She sipped her whiskey, her jaw tightening as she glanced at Edward, who still hadn't moved.

"Wake up, Edward," she said softly, almost to herself. "Before she consumes you, too."

※

The gallery's atmosphere was electric, the vibrant canvases on the walls seeming to pulse with the charged energy of the unfolding drama. Joan's words hung in the air like a poised blade, sharp and waiting to strike.

Dorothy tilted her head, her laugh cutting through the tension like a knife cloaked in velvet. It was a sound that was equal parts charm and deflection. "Manipulate?" she repeated, arching a delicate brow. "My dear Joan, you make it sound so... calculated." Her eyes glinted, catching the gallery's stark lighting as she swirled the champagne in her glass. "I simply offer what people already desire. Is it a crime to inspire?"

Joan stepped closer, her fiery hair catching the light like embers. "And what about the aftermath, Dorothy?" she countered, her voice low and unyielding. "The broken hearts, the shattered egos? Do you even notice the wreckage you leave behind? Or do you just keep walking, heels clicking over the pieces?"

Edward, standing a few steps away, visibly flinched. His champagne flute trembled in his hand, and his gaze darted nervously between the two women. Confusion clouded his features, mingled with something darker—a dawning realization that he hadn't yet found the words for.

Dorothy's gaze flicked toward him, a brief crack in her armor revealing something softer, something almost tender. But it was gone in an instant, replaced by the unflappable confidence she wore like a second skin. "Life is messy, Joan," she said, her voice calm but with an edge of warning. "Art is messy. Surely you, of all people, understand that."

Edward's voice broke through, tentative but tinged with strain. "Dorothy," he began, swallowing hard. "I... I don't understand. What is she talking about?"

Dorothy turned to him, her expression softening in a way that felt almost rehearsed. "Edward, darling—"

But Joan wasn't finished. "She's talking about the way you let her consume you," Joan interrupted, her words razor-sharp. "How she draws people in, feeds off their admiration, their devotion. And when she's had her fill? She leaves. Always looking for the next bright light to extinguish."

Edward's face paled, his paint-stained fingers tightening around the stem of his glass. He looked at Dorothy, his voice trembling. "Is that true?" he asked, the question breaking like glass between them. "Am I just… another muse to you? Another name on a list?"

Dorothy's lips parted, but for a moment, no words came. Mordecai, watching from the periphery, saw it—the flicker of vulnerability, the faintest shadow of regret crossing her face before she smoothed it away.

"Edward," she said finally, her voice gentle but steady. "You're an artist. You see the world in all its beautiful, chaotic complexity. Our connection, it's part of that. Part of the beauty we create together."

Edward's brow furrowed, his lips pressing into a thin line. "I thought," he began, his voice thick with emotion, "I thought we had something real. Something… special."

Dorothy reached out, her fingers just barely grazing his arm. "We do, Edward," she said softly. "In its own way, we do."

Joan let out a quiet, derisive laugh. "In its own way?" she repeated, shaking her head. "You really are something, Dorothy. Always leaving just enough hope to keep them tethered to you."

Mordecai watched Dorothy closely. For all her poise, her unflappable charm, there was a tightness in her jaw, a flicker of something raw behind her eyes. The Dorothy he knew would have deflected, laughed off Joan's accusations with a biting quip. But now, standing under the gallery lights, she seemed… unsure. It was like watching a dancer falter mid-step, unsure whether to keep moving or take a bow.

Edward took a shaky step back, setting his glass on a nearby table.

His expression was a storm of emotions—hurt, confusion, and the bitter sting of betrayal. "I need some air," he mumbled, turning toward the exit.

"Edward, wait—" Dorothy began, but the words died on her lips as he disappeared into the crowd.

The silence that followed was deafening. Joan crossed her arms, her gaze unwavering. "There it is," she said quietly, almost to herself. "The moment the curtain falls."

Dorothy's shoulders squared, the crack in her facade barely visible as she turned to face Joan. "Is this what you wanted, Joan?" she asked, her voice low and steady. "To tear me down in front of him? To make him question everything?"

Joan didn't flinch. "I didn't have to tear you down, Dorothy," she said. "You've been doing that all by yourself."

Mordecai stepped forward then, his calm presence a balm against the rising tension. "Perhaps this conversation is best continued elsewhere," he suggested, his voice steady but firm. His hand rested lightly on Dorothy's arm, guiding her away from Joan's piercing gaze.

Dorothy allowed herself to be led, but as they moved through the crowd, Mordecai felt her tension, her unspoken thoughts simmering just beneath the surface. He glanced at her, his voice low. "You don't have to pretend with me, Dorothy."

Her laugh was soft, almost bitter. "And what would I be without the pretense, Mordecai?" she murmured. "Would there be anything left?"

Mordecai didn't answer. He simply stayed by her side, a steady presence as the weight of the evening pressed down around them.

Dorothy's tan skin flushed, Joan's words reverberating through her mind like echoes in an empty hall. The low hum of the gallery lights buzzed faintly in her ears, blending with the rising tide of doubt and anger swirling in her chest. Her fingers tightened around the stem of her champagne flute, knuckles whitening as she steadied herself. The faces of those she'd touched—Edward, Elodie, Joan—flickered through her mind like a slideshow, their emotions a kaleidoscope of longing, frustration, and raw hunger. Each image hit her like a punch, a reminder of the threads she had pulled and the knots she had left behind.

"I never meant to—" Dorothy began, her voice faltering. She swallowed hard, her usual playful lilt conspicuously absent. The words tasted unfamiliar, foreign on her tongue. "It's not as simple as you make it sound, Joan."

Joan's sharp gaze lingered for a moment longer, but she didn't press further. Perhaps she sensed the momentary fragility in Dorothy, a chink in the armor she so carefully maintained. Instead, Joan stepped back, her silence cutting deeper than words could.

From the edge of the room, Mordecai observed the interplay, his keen eyes missing none of the tension that rippled between Dorothy and Joan. He moved with quiet purpose, his presence beside Dorothy both grounding and deliberate.

"Perhaps we should find somewhere quieter to discuss this," Mordecai murmured, his voice low enough to be intimate but loud enough to cut through the charged silence. His hand ghosted over the small of Dorothy's back, a steadying gesture that carried no expectation—only understanding.

Dorothy hesitated, glancing back at Joan, whose emerald eyes still burned with unspoken accusations. With a quiet nod, Dorothy allowed Mordecai to guide her away from the gallery's pulsing heart, the weight of her unspoken words following her like a shadow.

They found refuge in a secluded alcove, tucked away from the vibrant conversations and the low saxophone melodies filtering through the air. Here, the world softened, the sharp edges of the gallery receding into muted hues. Dorothy's breath hitched as Mordecai handed her a fresh flute of champagne, his steady presence somehow both unnerving and comforting.

"Do you ever wonder," Mordecai began softly, his piercing gaze holding hers, "what lies beneath all that fire?"

Dorothy tilted her head, her lips curving into a faint, tired smile. "Perhaps it's not fire at all, Mordecai," she replied, her voice quieter now. "Perhaps it's just smoke."

The words hung between them, heavy with the weight of unspoken truths. Mordecai's fingers brushed hers as he took the glass from her hand, setting it aside on a nearby ledge. The touch was fleeting yet charged, a deliberate pause in the storm of her thoughts. A shiver rippled through her, one she couldn't entirely blame on the room's draft.

"And what if it's neither?" Mordecai pressed, his voice dipping lower, intimate in a way that felt almost too raw. "What if it's something entirely different—something you've been running from all this time?"

Dorothy's breath caught in her throat, and for a moment, she couldn't meet his eyes. She turned her gaze to the champagne flute, watching the bubbles rise in delicate spirals. "I don't run," she whispered, but even she heard the hollow note in her words.

"Don't you?" Mordecai's hand found hers again, his thumb tracing slow, deliberate circles on her palm. His tone wasn't accusatory, but the challenge in his words was undeniable. "You weave these intricate webs, Dorothy. But have you ever stopped to consider that you might be the one truly caught?"

Dorothy's head snapped up, her eyes narrowing at his observation. But there was no malice in Mordecai's expression, only an almost maddeningly gentle curiosity. That gentleness, she realized, was more disarming than any sharp critique.

"I give people what they want," she said finally, her voice steadier now. "Is that so terrible?"

"And what about what you want?" Mordecai countered, his fingers still tracing her skin. "Beyond the thrill of the chase, beyond the power of seduction. What do you truly desire?"

The question lingered, heavier than champagne bubbles and sharper than Joan's earlier barbs. Dorothy turned away, her gaze falling on a vibrant abstract painting across the room. Its chaotic strokes of red and gold seemed to mirror the turmoil in her heart.

"I don't know," she admitted at last, her voice barely audible. "Maybe I never have."

Mordecai stepped closer, his voice soft but resolute. "It's okay not to know, Dorothy. But maybe it's time to stop running long enough to find out."

For a long moment, Dorothy didn't respond. Her fingers tightened slightly around his, as though anchoring herself to something real. When she finally turned back to him, her eyes shimmered with an emotion she couldn't name—perhaps gratitude, perhaps fear, perhaps something in between.

"Do you ever get tired of being the one with all the answers?" she asked, a faint smile ghosting across her lips.

Mordecai chuckled softly, the sound warm and reassuring. "No one has all the answers, my dear. But the right questions can take us a long way."

Dorothy nodded, her grip on his hand loosening but not entirely letting go. The storm in her chest settled, if only slightly, as she let his words sink in. And for the first time in what felt like years, she allowed herself to wonder what it might feel like to stop running.

꙰

Dorothy's eyes narrowed, a flash of defiance sparking in their depths as she squared herself against Mordecai's unwavering gaze. "And what would you know about being caught, Mordecai?" Her voice was sharp, cutting through the quiet of the alcove. "You, who always stands at the edges, observing but never truly engaging?"

Mordecai tilted his head, his lips curving into a wry smile that carried the weight of knowing far more than he let on. "Perhaps that's exactly why I can see it so clearly in you." He stepped closer, the space between them tightening, his presence both steady and unyielding. His fingers brushed hers again, intertwining slowly, deliberately. The gesture was intimate but layered—comforting and challenging in equal measure. "You create these elaborate dances of desire, Dorothy. But at what cost?"

Her instinctive response was to pull away, and she did, her arms crossing defensively as if to shield herself. "I give people what they want," she said, her tone clipped. "Is that so terrible?"

Mordecai let the silence hang for a moment, studying her, his expression unreadable. When he finally spoke, his voice was gentle but unflinching. "And what about what *you* want, Dorothy?" The question landed like a blow, a truth she wasn't prepared to face. "Beyond the thrill of the chase, beyond the power of seduction. What do you truly desire?"

Dorothy turned sharply, her gaze falling on a vibrant abstract painting mounted on the wall. Its chaotic strokes of red and gold seemed to pulsate under the gallery lights, mirroring the tempest inside her. She opened her mouth to respond, but the words faltered, her usual quick wit failing her for the first time in recent memory. "I..." she began, then stopped, her voice trailing into the void of her uncertainty.

Mordecai's voice broke the silence, low and steady. "It's okay not to have all the answers," he murmured, stepping closer. His proximity was comforting but unsettling, a reminder of his ability to see through her carefully constructed facade. "But perhaps it's time to start asking the right questions."

The weight of unspoken truths thickened the air around them, and for a moment, Dorothy felt suspended in time, caught between her instinct to deflect and the uncomfortable allure of vulnerability.

Finally, she turned to him, her eyes shimmering with unshed tears she didn't dare let fall. Her voice was steady, but soft, almost a whisper. "I think... I think it's time for me to go."

Mordecai nodded, a faint smile ghosting across his lips. There was no argument in his eyes, only understanding. "Where will you go?"

"Paris," she said simply, the word landing with a sense of inevitability. Her lips curved into a small, genuine smile, one of gratitude and perhaps a touch of relief. "I need... space. Time to reflect."

Mordecai's expression softened, a rare glimpse of something close to tenderness flickering across his features. "Paris will suit you," he said, his voice warm. "And maybe this time, it'll give you more than just a backdrop for your games."

Dorothy chuckled softly, shaking her head. "Thank you, Mordecai. For being the mirror I didn't know I needed."

As they made their way out of the gallery together, Dorothy felt a strange and conflicting tide of emotions washing over her. Pride in the chaos she'd left in her wake, a touch of melancholy for the connections she was leaving behind, and an unfamiliar spark of anticipation for what lay ahead.

***

The Eurostar terminal was a cacophony of movement—departures and reunions blending into a chaotic symphony. Yet Dorothy moved through the crowd with a quiet grace, her designer luggage trailing behind her like a loyal shadow.

As she approached the platform, her reflection caught her eye in the glass doors. She paused, taking herself in—the luminous skin, the shadowed eyes, the faint trace of a smile that didn't quite reach her lips. A study in contrasts, much like the life she'd so meticulously cultivated.

When the train began to board, Dorothy stepped forward, her heels clicking softly against the polished floors. The moment she crossed the threshold of the train car, she glanced back one final time.

Mordecai stood at the edge of the platform, his tall frame relaxed but his gaze fixed on her. Their eyes locked, and in that silent exchange, a thousand unspoken promises hung in the air.

Dorothy felt the familiar thrill of excitement spark in her chest, but this time it carried something new—a quiet, persistent ache. The possibility of genuine change.

As the train pulled away, Dorothy settled into her seat by the window. The cityscape of London blurred into the distance, and for the first time in years, Dorothy allowed herself a moment of stillness. The chase would always call to her, but perhaps, she thought, there was room for something more. Something deeper.

Paris awaited, and with it, whatever the next chapter of her story might hold.

🌸

The train's doors hissed shut, sealing Dorothy inside. Mordecai stood motionless on the platform, his eyes fixed on her silhouette through the tinted glass. As the Eurostar began to glide away, he felt a complex tapestry of emotions weaving through him.

"Au revoir, ma chère Dorothy," he murmured, his voice barely audible above the station's din.

The train picked up speed, becoming a blur of sleek metal and light. Mordecai's gaze remained locked on it until it vanished into the tunnel, carrying with it a woman who had irrevocably altered his world.

He turned away from the tracks, his mind awash with memories of Dorothy's laugh, the fierce glint in her eyes, the vulnerability she'd shown in rare, unguarded moments. The station bustled around him, a microcosm of human connection and separation.

"Desire is its own art form," Mordecai mused aloud, his words swallowed by the cacophony surrounding him. He pulled out his well-worn map of London, tracing the routes they'd taken together with a finger. "And like all art, it leaves both creator and subject irrevocably altered."

His phone buzzed – a message from Dorothy. "Already missing London's chaos. Paris has big shoes to fill. x"

Mordecai smiled, a bittersweet twinge in his chest. He typed back: "The chaos misses you too. Don't let Paris tame you entirely."

As he pocketed his phone, Mordecai reflected on the intricate dance of desire, power, and intimacy they'd shared. In this hyper-connected world, distance meant little. Dorothy's influence would linger, a digital ghost haunting the streets of London, the art galleries, the quiet corners where they'd shared secrets.

"What now, old friend?" he asked his map, feeling both liberated and unmoored. The city sprawled before him, full of possibility and lingering echoes of Dorothy's presence. Whatever came next, Mordecai knew one thing for certain – he would never see the world quite the same way again.

EPILOGUE

Months later, in a dimly lit Parisian café, Dorothy sipped her espresso, the city humming with life around her. Mordecai's voice echoed in her thoughts, a constant reminder of the boundaries she had crossed and the lessons she had learned. London had left its mark on her, and yet, the world still stretched out before her—an endless canvas of desire and discovery.

AFTERWORD

Writing *Velvet Entanglements* was an exploration of the delicate balance between power and vulnerability, the allure of intimacy, and the complexities of connection in a modern world. I hope this story resonates with you, offering both a sensual escape and a moment of introspection.

Thank you for joining me on this journey. If you enjoyed *Velvet Entanglements,* please consider leaving a review—it helps immensely and means the world to me.

ACKNOWLEDGEMENT

Thank you to my friends and family who inspire me every day with their resilience and love. To the readers who take a chance on my stories—you are the heart of my writing journey. And finally, to the daring souls who find beauty in vulnerability, this one's for you.

ABOUT THE AUTHOR

Fiona Harvey

Fiona Harvey is a storyteller who revels in exploring the complexities of human desire, connection, and power. Drawing inspiration from her travels, artistic endeavors, and life experiences, Fiona creates narratives that blend sensuality with introspection. When she's not weaving tales of passion and intrigue, she enjoys yoga, tarot reading, and finding beauty in the ordinary.

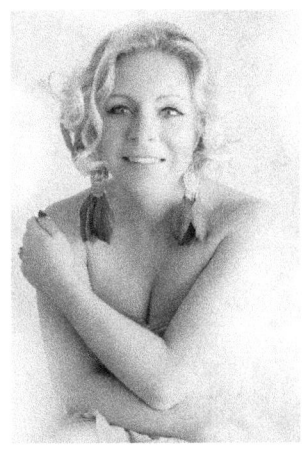

www.ingramcontent.com/pod-product-compliance
Lightning Source LLC
Chambersburg PA
CBHW071059240526
45471CB00016B/2157